THE RUCKSACK WE CARRY
A FIELD MANUAL FOR VETERANS AND FIRST RESPONDERS

STEVE LITTLEFIELD

LITTLEFIELD
PRESS

The Rucksack We Carry
A Field Manual for Veterans and First Responders

First Edition

Printed in the United States of America

ISBN: 979-8-9939859-6-1 (Paperback)
ISBN: 979-8-9939859-3-0 (Hardcover)
ISBN: 979-8-9939859-1-6 (E-Book)

Library of Congress Control Number: 2026910842
A catalog record for this book is available from the Library of Congress

Edited by Chris Evans

Contributions by Lauren Littlefield, LICSW; Christopher Bean, LMHC; Lori Kovalski, LMHC; Melissa Shea, LMHC

Cover design by Steve Littlefield

Published by Littlefield Press: Halifax, Massachusetts

This book is a work of nonfiction. Some names and identifying details have been changed to protect individuals' privacy. The views expressed in this book are those of the author and do not necessarily reflect the views of any agency, department, or organization with which the author has been affiliated.

Disclaimer: This book is not a substitute for professional mental health care, diagnosis, or treatment. It is intended to share perspectives and practical tools drawn from service, leadership, and lived experiences.

If you are in crisis or believe you may be a danger to yourself or others, seek immediate professional help, call 988, or contact local emergency services.

TABLE OF CONTENTS

For the ones who stood watch.
And for those still carrying the weight.

"Out of suffering have emerged the strongest souls.

The most massive characters are seared with scars."

KHALIL GIBRAN

AUTHOR'S NOTE

I'm not a doctor. I don't have a PhD, and I'm not here to diagnose you, analyze your childhood, or tell you how you "should" feel.

I'm writing this because I've lived with the weight that comes from service, and I've watched too many good men and women carry that same weight, quietly convinced that struggling meant they were weak, broken, or failing.

That belief has been ingrained in our culture for generations.

After World War I, soldiers returned home changed by what was then labeled *shell shock*. They shook, froze, panicked, dissociated, and couldn't sleep. Instead of being treated as injured, many were labeled fragile, cowardly, or morally defective. Some were even accused of betraying their country. Treatments were often harsh and punitive, designed to force compliance rather than offer understanding.[1]

The goal wasn't healing—it was correction.

The message was simple: If you can't handle it, you're the problem.

That message was wrong then, and it's wrong now.

Today, we understand that trauma, responsibility, and chronic stress change the brain and can keep the nervous system in a constant state of overdrive. These reactions aren't a failure of character. They are very normal human responses to very abnormal experiences.[2]

And yet, the shame remains. We know better, but we still fall back into the same lies.

We reward endurance over honesty. We praise people for pushing through without asking what it costs them. We treat silence like professionalism—and struggle like a personal flaw.

Guilt keeps the cycle going:

> *"I shouldn't feel this way."*
> *"Others have it worse."*
> *"I don't deserve help."*
> *"I don't want to be a burden."*

These are conditioned thoughts. They come from a culture that ties worth to performance, composure, and sacrifice—and teaches us to hide anything that threatens those traits.

This book rejects the idea that silence equals strength or that suffering in isolation should be commended. It challenges the belief that you should be able to take care of everything and everyone, all the time.

You can't.

We are not built for isolation. We are wired for connection—for support, shared understanding, friendship, and love.

If the weight stays with you after the uniform comes off...
If you've ever felt guilty for struggling...
If you've ever felt ashamed for needing help...

This book is for you.

We've come too far to keep carrying the mistakes of the past forward.

And we've buried too many brothers and sisters to keep pretending that silence is strength.

For me, it all traces back to a single date on the calendar.

For you, your story is your own—unique, complicated, painful, meaningful, and everything in between. It is what makes you who you are.

And that, in and of itself, is beautiful and worth honoring.

INTRODUCTION

There are certain days that divide our lives into two parts:

Before and After.

We don't always recognize them when they happen. Most begin like any other day. The sun rises. People move through their daily routines. The world keeps turning.

But on this day, the world stopped.

On the morning of September 11, 2001, I was sitting in a car dealership waiting room when American Airlines Flight 11 struck the North Tower at 8:46 am.

What followed didn't feel real:

People leaping from the Twin Towers.
Buildings collapsing into themselves.
Smoke pouring from the Pentagon.
Flight 93 crashing into a field in Shanksville, Pennsylvania.

On September 12, I was scheduled to leave for Army Basic Combat Training. I was only nineteen, already questioning whether I had made the right decision to join the military. Now, there were a million more questions...

Two of those planes had departed from Boston's Logan Airport—the same one I was scheduled to fly out from the very next morning. The rest of the day unfolded in stunned silence—waiting, packing, watching, and wondering what came next.

My flight was canceled. All air travel was shut down.

When I finally left on September 17, I stepped into a new Army—and a world that no longer resembled the one I had grown up in.

The attacks on the World Trade Center and the Pentagon didn't just change America's foreign policy or alter the landscape of the world we live in. More personally, they set into motion a chain of events that would shape the next quarter-century of my life.

That chain of events pulled me across continents and into roles I never could have imagined.

It took me to Iraq in 2004 with the 42nd Division Artillery, and again to Afghanistan in 2010 with the 101st Field Artillery Regiment. The final eight years of my military career, including some trying times during the COVID-19 pandemic, were spent in the 179th and 180th Engineer Detachments, a firefighting unit where I served as Commander and Fire Marshal until my retirement in 2026.

Beyond the military, I've served as a corrections officer, a police officer in a busy tourist town on Cape Cod, and as the Veteran Service Officer for my hometown in Halifax, Massachusetts. In that role, I meet with veterans and their families, listen to their stories, and help them navigate systems designed to support them—often long after the uniform comes off.

First responder and military cultures have shaped my life and career.

Along the way, I've worn a lot of other hats: husband, father, baseball coach, entrepreneur, and graduate student in mental health counseling.

I am also someone who has lived and struggled with chronic post-traumatic stress disorder (PTSD), anxiety, and depression. I've spent over two decades trying to make sense of it, and I still don't have it all figured out—not even close. But with God's blessing of each new day, I try to move forward.

I am no Medal of Honor recipient, Army Ranger, or Special Forces operator—certainly no Hollywood hero. I'm just a regular soldier who did my job and tried to take care of the people around me—just like most of us.

And like most of us, the experiences that get under our skin aren't always the ones made for movies. They're the daily grind, the constant pressure, and sometimes the unthinkable moments we wish we could forget, but never really can.

This book is meant to serve as a **mental health field manual** for those of us who wear the uniform.

For those unfamiliar with an Army Field Manual, it's a no-nonsense guide meant to be used—not necessarily admired. This book could have been 500 pages long, but that would defeat the purpose. It's meant to be a tool you can carry with you, pull from when needed, and apply in real life.

At the end of each chapter, you'll find _Action Steps_ and _Field Notes_ designed to give you practical tools you can utilize immediately.

While this is written with the military, law enforcement, fire services, and medical communities in mind, the tools here apply to anyone carrying the weight of stress, trauma, or burnout.

When the COVID-19 pandemic began, I was deployed with a Massachusetts National Guard State Response Team called Task Force Medical. I was responsible for coordinating testing and health-care support for thousands of elderly and medically fragile patients in nursing homes and long-term care facilities across the Commonwealth.

For nearly three months, I couldn't sleep in my own home—even though I was only an hour away. When I had time, I'd buy groceries, leave them on the doorstep at the house, and wave to my wife and kids through the glass before turning around and leaving again.

Those early months of COVID carried a kind of weight that's hard to put into words—fear, uncertainty, and responsibility all stacked at once.

Our teams watched a lot of people die on that mission.

And while we were carrying that, our own families were at home struggling without us.

> That kind of weight sticks around—
> whether you admit it or not.

It was also during this time that I started thinking about mental health differently—less about the clinical side, and more about how responsibility, stress, trauma, and the quiet accumulation of pressure build over time. Clinicians I admire, like Dr. John Delony, spoke about these things in plain language.[1] He helped me put words to what I was carrying—not just during the pandemic, but from the 20-plus years of service before it. This period also marked the point when I realized I didn't just want to *understand* these experiences—I wanted to *do* something about it after my military career.

What stuck with me was that we all move through life carrying different and unique weight that only grows heavier over time.

For those of us in the military and first responder professions, a normal backpack doesn't hold that kind of weight. We carry ours in a rucksack—the metaphor I will use throughout this book.

Unlike an everyday backpack, a rucksack is built to carry heavy loads over long journeys—much like the professional lives we lead. Over time, even the best-fitting rucksack will dig into your shoulders and strain your back if you never stop to adjust it.

Our professions teach us how to carry this weight. What it doesn't teach us is how to _set it down_.

This book isn't about making that weight disappear. That's not possible in the professions we chose.

It's about learning to recognize when the weight is becoming too much, how to redistribute it, and when to set it down or let someone else carry it—so you can keep moving forward without being crushed underneath it.

AUDIENCE, USE, AND SAFETY

This book is primarily written from a military perspective, but the weight we discuss is not unique to any one uniform.

The tools, language, and concepts in these pages are intended for anyone in high-stress, high-responsibility roles—law enforcement, fire services, EMS, corrections, medicine, and other professions where exposure to cumulative trauma, loss, and chronic pressure is part of the job.

While the cultures, policies, and risks may differ, the human cost of carrying that weight over time is remarkably similar.

> That said, no two professions—or departments—
> operate the same way.

Policies around confidentiality, fitness for duty, documentation, and mandatory reporting vary by profession, state, agency, and even individual department.

Some readers may have access to peer support teams, chaplains, embedded clinicians, or employee assistance programs. Others work in environments where trust is harder to come by, and discretion matters more.

Use what applies to your situation and adapt as necessary. If there is any doubt, follow your local policies and chain of command.

The idea of stress accumulating over time isn't something new. Variations of this metaphor exist across psychology, leadership, and everyday life. What follows is a way to understand it within the context of military and first responder experience.

It's a practical guide to help you recognize what you're carrying, understand how it's affecting you, and make informed decisions about when and how to seek or offer support before the rucksack breaks.

This book is not a substitute for professional mental health care and does not override medical advice, departmental policies, or legal requirements.

IF YOU'RE IN IMMEDIATE DANGER

This needs to be stated as clearly as possible:

If you are in immediate danger or having thoughts of suicide, call or text **988** (Veterans, press 1), contact your department's Emergency Assistance Program, or use local emergency resources *immediately*.

If you are with someone who is at risk, stay with them. If possible, remove access to any lethal means. Contact on-duty leadership and emergency services.

Don't assume that someone else will take care of it.

As the old saying goes, sometimes things are "not by our hand, but in our lap." Act accordingly, and don't downplay the situation.

Reaching out in those moments is a duty and responsibility.

FIELD NOTES

This book is about naming the weight you're carrying in your rucksack, recognizing when it's getting heavier than it should, and using the right mix of personal tools, peer support, and professional resources to keep going without losing yourself in the process.

You don't have to do it all alone. You don't have to wait until things are falling apart. And you don't have to be ashamed of needing support in work that asks so much of you.

**This book exists to help you stay in the fight.
Whole, present, and alive.**

THE RUCKSACK

"It's not the load that breaks you down; it's the way you carry it."

LOU HOLTZ

If you've spent any time in a high-stress profession—military, law enforcement, fire services, corrections, EMS, dispatch, healthcare, or countless others—you are carrying the proverbial rucksack. You can't see it, and it doesn't always weigh the same. Some days, it feels like nothing. Other days, it feels so heavy you can barely stand under it. But it is always there. You can't toss it away just because the shift ends, the call clears, or the deployment is over.

That's the life we chose.

That rucksack is filled with experiences. Some are small and light—the kind you hardly notice. Others are heavier, pressing against you when you least expect it or when you really don't have time to deal with them. And then there are the massive, earth-shattering events that change your world and leave a mark with every step.

Over the course of a life and career, the weight shifts constantly. Much of it is beyond our control. The worst memories aren't the ones we invite in. They're the ambush calls (literally and figuratively), random losses, trauma, and tragedies that slip into the rucksack without permission.

You can have the best practices in place and still have moments crash through your defenses. They settle deep in the bottom of the rucksack, and their weight changes the way you move forward.

To begin making sense of it, think of the weight you carry in three categories: **pebbles, rocks, and boulders.**

PEBBLES – THE EVERYDAY WEAR AND TEAR

These are the small stresses and frustrations that come with the job. They seem minor, but over time, they add up. Endless forms to fill out. Never-ending radio chatter or medical codes. The 2 a.m. call that wakes you for the third night in a row.

Alone, pebbles don't seem like much. The problem is their persistence. They sneak into your rucksack every day. Soon, the straps start digging into your shoulders. The weight isn't crushing, but it's constant, and that can wear down even the strongest back.

**Most people aren't crushed by a single boulder.
They're buried under a lifetime of pebbles.**

Here are some additional examples of the pebbles we carry around:

- **Military:** Endless PowerPoint briefings, broken equipment that never seems to get fixed, always being away when the family needs you, or yet another "mandatory fun" event.
- **Law Enforcement:** Another call for a dog barking at the same address, the same criminals repeatedly committing the same crimes, hours of report writing, or radio traffic that never seems to stop—especially right before your shift is over.
- **Fire Service:** The 4 a.m. call for a malfunctioning carbon monoxide detector again, after you just got back to sleep, and trucks that are out of service due to budget cuts.
- **EMS:** Transporting a patient who just wanted a ride to the hospital cafeteria, or the one who's had leg pain for three months and decides to call an ambulance at 1:30 a.m.
- **Healthcare:** Charting until your eyes are crossed or dealing with insurance authorizations that somehow take longer than the actual patient care.

ROCKS – THE CALLS YOU CAN'T SHAKE

Rocks are different. These are heavier incidents that hit harder. They don't enter your rucksack every day—but when they do, they stay with you for a while.

These are the calls that return after the adrenaline fades—when the station goes quiet or when you're alone in your truck on the drive home. It might be someone you couldn't help. It might be the sound of a grieving family, or the silence that follows when the chaos ends.

You can still function with rocks in your rucksack. You go to work and keep moving, but you feel them with you. They remind you that not all the weight you carry can be shrugged off.

Here are some examples of what rocks in the rucksack might look like:

- **Military:** A convoy that didn't come back the way it left, performing casualty notification duties and informing a family of an active-duty death.
- **Law Enforcement:** Telling a family that their loved one isn't coming home, the "dead-on-arrival" calls, or an in-service accident or injury.
- **Fire Service:** Pulling someone from a fire only to realize they didn't make it.
- **EMS:** A cardiac arrest that didn't respond, no matter how hard you tried.
- **Healthcare:** Sitting with a patient as they get life-changing news and seeing their face fall in agony.

BOULDERS – THE LIFE ALTERING MOMENTS

Then there are the boulders. These are moments so massive they change the way you carry everything else. A boulder doesn't just add weight. It changes your stride, your posture, and your pace. It reshapes how you see the world.

Once a boulder lands in your rucksack, you can't ever really take it out. What you can do is learn to balance it, share the load, and keep walking without it bringing you to your knees.

Examples of boulders may include:

- **Military:** Losing a friend or teammate in combat, experiencing military sexual trauma.
- **Law Enforcement:** The day you're forced to draw your weapon—and use it.
- **Fire Service:** A multi-fatality fire where you knew people inside but couldn't get to them.
- **EMS:** Responding to a call involving your own family member or close friend, or caring for a child who isn't going to make it.
- **Healthcare:** A mass-casualty event where no matter how hard you worked, there just weren't enough resources to save everyone.

This isn't a complete list, and it's not meant to be. The weight isn't the event itself, but rather how it lands in your mind and body. Similar events will weigh differently for each individual.

Psychiatrist Bessel van der Kolk explains that trauma isn't just stored in the mind. It also lives in the body, influencing how you move, breathe, and respond to stress.[1] That's why you can feel fine one moment and suddenly be pulled back into a traumatic experience.

Your body remembers, even when your mind believes you have moved on. Conceptually, you may even understand this—yet your body still reacts as if the threat is present.

Most of us struggle to maintain our mental health, which is understandable. For generations, we've been conditioned to believe we should be able to handle everything and take care of everyone—all the time.

My wife is a Licensed Independent Clinical Social Worker (LICSW), and one of the main reasons I'm standing here today. She puts it this way: We'll see a doctor immediately for a broken bone or the flu, yet somehow convince ourselves that our mental health can wait—that we can handle it on our own.

We'll tape an ankle or head to the urgent care clinic for strep, but when it comes to mental wounds, we let them sit, fester, and rot—convincing ourselves that we can handle it while quietly bleeding out inside. Over time, we start telling ourselves certain stories about the weight we carry.

> **Myth:** "I've seen worse. This is nothing."
> **Reality Check:** Trauma isn't a scoreboard. Just because
>   you've seen worse doesn't erase what you've been
>   through. Every incident can leave a pebble or a rock.
>   Over time, they pile up.

Myth: *"I'm fine as long as I'm working."*
Reality Check: Work can distract you, but it isn't a cure. If your only coping strategy is staying busy, you're running on borrowed time. Burnout sneaks up quietly, and when it hits, it doesn't just take you out of the fight—it can steal your ability to enjoy the rest of your life. Rest is essential.

Myth: *"If I ignore it for long enough, it will probably just go away."*
Reality Check: Been there. Done that. Got the T-shirt. Ignoring trauma is like neglecting an infection—it doesn't heal, it gets worse. It will surface eventually, and usually at the worst possible time.

Myth: *"I can't un-see it, so what's the point?"*
Reality Check: True—you can't erase a memory. But you can change how it lives in your mind. With the right tools, those images lose their power to hijack your thoughts and ruin your day. It isn't about forgetting. It's about making peace with the fact that it happened.

Myth: *"I don't want to burden anyone with my problems."*
Reality Check: You are not a burden, and you are worth being well. Letting someone help gives them the chance to step up for you the same way you've stepped up for others.

Myth: *"I should be able to handle this on my own by now."*
Reality Check: Healing isn't a straight path, and it doesn't follow a schedule. Some things take months. Others take years. Setting a deadline for recovery only adds pressure and shame—neither of which helps you heal.

Myth: *"Everyone else seems to be fine, so I must be over-reacting."*
Reality Check: You can't see inside someone else's rucksack. They might be carrying just as much weight, but hiding it the same way you are.

Myth: *"I don't have time for therapy or self-care."*
Reality Check: You must make the time. If you don't prioritize self-care now, you'll deal with it later—usually when something breaks down physically or mentally.

If any of this sounds like you, you are not broken.

You are human.

But you do need to start unpacking before the rucksack snaps. You can't carry this weight forever without adjusting the straps, redistributing the weight, or occasionally passing it to someone else.

My hope is that this book helps you do exactly that—with honesty, humility, and strength.

**Pebbles add up. Rocks shift the balance.
Boulders can change everything.
And every rucksack has a limit.**

CHAPTER 1 ACTION STEP: PEBBLES, ROCKS & BOULDERS

- List your pebbles, rocks, and boulders
- Reflect, in writing, how each still shows up in your life

A note on journaling: Even if you never show your writing to another soul, the act of putting thoughts on paper can be therapeutic. When thoughts stay in your head, they tend to loop—replaying the same scenes, the same "what-ifs," and the same negative self-talk until they feel heavier than they really are. Writing interrupts that loop. It forces your brain to slow down, shape those feelings, and organize the chaos into words. That process alone can often make things seem more manageable.

Research on expressive writing indicates that journaling can reduce stress, improve mood, and even alleviate physical symptoms associated with anxiety and trauma, in some cases leading to measurable improvements in both mental and physical health.[2] It's like taking some of the weight from the rucksack and putting it on the ground for a while. The load is still there, and you're going to have to pick it back up, but it's no longer overwhelming. And if you read your writing back to yourself, you may see patterns, triggers, and progress you might not have noticed in the moment.

CHAPTER 1 FIELD NOTES:

Everyone's rucksack is different, but everyone is carrying something. The longer you pretend yours is empty, the more likely it is to break you down. Naming what you're carrying is the first step in making it lighter.

But naming the weight isn't enough. At the heart of the rucksack is the **frame**. Without it, the pack collapses under the load. The frame doesn't remove the weight—it distributes it and keeps it from crushing you.

Your mental health works the same way. You need a frame strong enough to hold the weight. That's where the **RUCKSACK Framework** comes in, setting the foundation for the rest of this book.

THE RUCKSACK
FRAMEWORK

Recognize The Weight

Name what you're carrying: pebbles, rocks, and boulders. If you won't admit it's heavy, you'll never adjust the straps.

Unpack Early

Don't wait for the breakdown. Small conversations now prevent bigger crises later.

Check On Your People

If someone seems off, say something. It doesn't have to be perfect. Watching each other's backs includes the hidden battles.

Keep Your Body Ready

Sleep. Exercise. Eat right. This is your foundation. Your nervous system is part of your gear.

Silence Makes It Heavier

Isolation and secrets add weight. Talking about it doesn't make you weak. It makes you stronger.

Ask For Reinforcements

Peer support. Leadership. Chaplains and Clergy. Professional Counselors. Calling for backup is a strategy, not surrender.

Culture Starts at the Top

Leaders set the tone and example in both words and actions. What leaders normalize becomes the standard.

Keep Carrying Together

The weight of the job doesn't get lighter. But we were never meant to carry it alone.

CHAPTER 2
IRAQ
LIFE ON A FORWARD OPERATING BASE

"The most important six inches on the battlefield is between your ears."

GEN JAMES MATTIS, U.S. MARINE CORPS

I raq, 2004-2005.

In my experience, life on a Forward Operating Base (FOB) wasn't the war-story highlight reel you see on YouTube or X. *"When's chow?"* was usually how you measured your day. Most of the time, it meant managing a constant undertone of anxiety and uncertainty while doing your job, whatever that job might be.

For me, that was at FOB Summerall in Northern Iraq, helping run the Tactical Operations Center (TOC) and managing a team of drone pilots who flew reconnaissance missions across our area of operations, searching for insurgent activity and improvised explosive devices (IEDs).

. . .

Anytime we left a hardened building, we had to put on "full kit"—Kevlar helmet, full body armor, and weapon and ammo at the ready. The threat level was always high.

It was a strange mix of boredom interrupted by sudden bursts of pure chaos. And boredom, as it often does, led to some questionable decisions—mostly harmless pranks or practical jokes to pass the time and ease the tension.

But every now and then, someone pushed the limit a little too far, like the day a couple of buddies decided to pop off a red smoke grenade for laughs. For context, a red smoke grenade is usually used for medical emergencies. Not boredom.

At first, it didn't seem like a big deal. A little smoke—a little chuckle.

Then, it kept going. And going.

What started as a small cloud turned into a thick wall of red smoke that swallowed the entire building and was visible across the entire base. From the outside, it probably looked like something had gone very, very wrong.

It was funny for about five seconds. The paperwork that followed wasn't.

Then, there were the moments that broke through the monotony and reminded you *exactly* where you were.

One morning in April 2005, an insurgent-launched 120mm rocket exploded about seventy-five yards from my position, which happened to be my bunk, where I was trying to get some sleep after the night shift. Thankfully, we had sandbagged those windows.

I still remember the 'whizz' as the round came in, the hiss of shrapnel through the air, the dirt and debris pelting the walls, and the ever-present Iraqi dust floating in the sunlight after being blasted off the floor and ceiling.

That moment is forever etched in my memory.

Every day, my mind cycled through the same questions:

"Is today the day?"
"Maybe the next rocket is the one that gets us."

Some of my friends joked that I would jump and startle whenever the rounds came in, almost daily. After a while, we could clearly distinguish the incoming rounds (bad guys) from the outgoing rounds (good guys). They seemed to get used to it. I never really did.

Maybe something was wrong with me—or maybe I just refused to adapt to almost getting blown up.

While I was in Iraq, a good friend of mine—Sergeant Michael J. Kelley from Scituate, Massachusetts—was killed in a similar indirect fire attack in Shkin, Afghanistan, while unloading equipment at a helicopter landing zone.[1]

He was assigned to Battery E (Target Acquisition Battery), 1st Battalion, 101st Field Artillery Regiment out of Rehoboth, Massachusetts. He was only 26 when he was killed in action.

We had served together on a Force Protection mission, pulling security at the Massachusetts Military Reservation (now Joint Base Cape Cod) after the attacks on 9/11 and my return from boot camp and advanced individual training.

Hearing about his death while I was in another war zone made me realize how random and unfair it all felt. A few of us in the unit were very close to Mike. We shared many good memories from our days on the Cape.

That loss added a new weight to my rucksack—one I carried throughout the rest of the deployment, and to some extent, still carry today.

I didn't understand it at the time, but I think Mike's death was when my rucksack started to get pretty heavy.

Yes, he was in Afghanistan, and I was in Iraq, but distance doesn't blunt that kind of loss. It hit me hard. One minute, I'm going through the motions of another day in the desert, and the next I'm staring at the ground trying to make sense of how a guy I trained with, laughed with, and trusted was gone.

It was a mix of grief, disbelief, and a kind of helpless rage that I had nowhere to channel.

But the mission didn't give me time to process any of this. We still had a job to do, and the base kept getting hit with mortars, rockets, and the ever-present threat of IEDs. It felt like the universe didn't give a shit that Mike was gone or that we were hurting. It just kept throwing more at us.

Relaxing was impossible. Every part of me stayed wound tight because the alternative felt like an inevitable disaster.

Yet—and this is hard to explain—I became more focused than ever. Almost obsessively dialed in. I wasn't just doing my job. I was locked into it with an intensity that made everything else seem wasteful. I was trying to control everything I possibly could in an environment that was out of control.

However, that kind of focus is not a recipe for peace.

> It wasn't calm.
> It wasn't controlled.
> **It was survival mode.**

But in that season, all I knew was that we could not afford to slip up.

> Not after losing Mike.

I was scanning constantly, waiting for the next explosion, the next alarm, the next thing trying to take us out. My body stayed on high alert for twelve straight months...

> And then I was back home, expected to drop my rucksack at
> the door as if it had never happened.

Environments like that condition our mind and body to live in a constant state of alert. Even after the deployment ends or the call clears, your system doesn't always get the message that the danger is over. The background hum of stress, the memories that surface out of nowhere, and the physical reactions in your body don't just disappear.

> They linger.

And if you don't learn how to recognize them, they start to shape your life in ways you may not even realize.

CHAPTER 2 ACTION STEP: NAMING YOUR FOB CONDITIONS

- Identify your current **FOB Conditions.** List three ongoing stressors (the constant hum in the background) and one acute event you can still feel in your body.
- Rate each on a **1-10 intensity** scale for today.
- Think about *where* you feel it in your body. Maybe it's in your gut or the center of your chest. Maybe it shows up as knots in your shoulders or recurring headaches. What does it feel like—sharp, dull, hot, cold, tingly?

Write it down.

CHAPTER 2 FIELD NOTES:

You can't control the mortars and rockets that land close. You can't control when things go sideways, or when a routine day turns into something you carry for the rest of your life. That was part of the reality in Iraq. But even in that environment, there were things I could control—routines, discipline, and checks and balances. The small things that kept me grounded when everything else felt unstable.

That same principle applies to what you carry after the fact. You can't erase what happened, but you can decide how you deal with it. Naming the weight matters. Ignoring it doesn't make it lighter—it just gives it more control. When you take the time to recognize what you're carrying, you take a piece of that control back. And in a world where so much is out of your hands, that means more than most people realize.

CHAPTER 3
AFGHANISTAN
SECONDS THAT LAST FOREVER

"War is the realm of chance."

CARL VON CLAUSEWITZ

I n 2010, I deployed again—this time to Afghanistan.

My official role was Battle Captain in the Joint Task Force Kabul Movement Control Center based at Camp Phoenix. Even as a Sergeant (not a Captain, as the title suggests), I was responsible for keeping the Movement Control Cell running. That meant tracking every convoy and patrol in our area of operations—over 7,000 in total throughout the deployment.

We supported the patrols in any way possible, including coordinating wreckers for broken-down vehicles, Explosive Ordnance Disposal (EOD) for roadside bombs, Quick Reaction Force (QRF) for enemy contact or urgent situations, or medical evacuations (MEDEVACs) when lives were at risk.

I can somewhat compare it to ground-based air traffic control. We used traditional radio communication and a GPS tracking system called the Blue Force Tracker (BFT) to exchange messages, send and receive situation reports (SITREPs), provide intelligence, issue traffic alerts, update personnel statuses, and deliver other relevant information.

I spent most of my time inside the wire (a Fobbit, as some would say), in what felt like a bubble of partial safety. Occasionally, I joined a small group of about a dozen soldiers to conduct partnership meetings with coalition forces, including Portuguese and Italian soldiers fighting alongside us. During these trips, I would usually man the M240B machine gun on our vehicle.

That shit was nerve-wracking.

I had immense respect for those who went outside the wire every day because they faced a different level of stress. That bubble of safety within the camp wasn't foolproof, but it offered a fragile sense of control and structure that didn't exist outside it.

On April 19, 2010, we lost Sergeant Robert J. Barrett, of Fall River, Massachusetts. He was only 20 years old, assigned to Battery A, 1st Battalion, 101st Field Artillery Regiment, based in Fall River, Massachusetts.[1]

He was a member of an Afghanistan National Army (ANA) mentor team based out of Camp Dubbs in southern Kabul. They traveled daily to Kabul International Airport to train Afghan soldiers in tactics, security, first aid, and fundamental military skills.

On that day, a suicide bomber wearing an explosive belt slipped into the group dressed as an Afghan Army soldier.

In a split second, he detonated the belt, tearing through the group, killing Sergeant Barrett and wounding several others. One moment, the team was conducting routine training, as they had many times before. The next, complete chaos. No warning, no escalation—just an eruption of evil and violence that left the team scrambling. Another reminder of how fragile the line is between normal and catastrophic—and how quickly a world can change.

In the heat of the moment, Barrett's team sent frantic messages to the Operations Center at Camp Dubbs, but Dubbs couldn't get the request through to the medical helicopter unit. Certain areas of the city experienced significant radio interference, especially during particular times of the day. As Murphy's Law would have it, this seemed to be one of those times. Camp Dubbs relayed the 9-LINE (the standardized form for this request, which included the necessary information to get the helicopter airborne) to us at Camp Phoenix.

Specifically, to me.

I remember that moment with complete clarity.

The buzz of operations seemed to fade away entirely. The background noise, side-chatter, keyboard clicks, and other radio transmissions—all went silent in my head. My heart began pounding, and my whole body felt flushed and warm—the rush you get when adrenaline floods your system. Every movement felt both insanely fast and impossibly slow. And this was nothing, *I mean nothing,* compared to what was happening at the scene.

I knew, before most people in the room knew, that Sergeant Barrett was already gone. There was something in the way they spoke that told me, but the process continued.

I read the first line of the 9-LINE, my voice steady, even though my hands were clammy on the radio handset. I confirmed the grid coordinates, one digit at a time, feeling the weight of how crucial it was that they be right. I relayed his medical condition, each code landing like a brick in my chest, knowing how real it was. It felt like forever to get through all nine lines, but I wasn't going to let one error make a terrible situation even worse.

Eventually, Sergeant Barrett was evacuated to Camp Phoenix in a military vehicle. He was gone. The MEDEVAC could not save him. When the helicopters did arrive at Camp Phoenix later to begin the long journey of bringing his body home, nearly the entire base attended a "ramp ceremony", where we honored the sacrifice that he had literally just made. I stayed in the Movement Control Center. Someone had to stay behind and keep it going. Missions were still running. I was numb.

Afterward, the heaviness across the base felt almost tangible:

Conversations quieted.
Movements slowed.
Everything seemed muffled.
Nothing felt real.

The kicker was that everyone still had a job to do the next day. Convoys rolled out of the gate, patrols conducted training, and operations continued.

The mission pressed on.

But there was a weight in the air—a shared understanding that no one needed to say out loud. We had just lost one of our own, and tomorrow we had to walk back into the same dangers that took him.

The quote at the beginning of the chapter never felt truer than it did on this day:

"War is the realm of chance."

Nothing about that day was predictable:

> An unthinkable tragedy.
> A great soldier's life—gone.
> A new father—gone.
> A brother, son, and friend—gone.

And the lives around him forever changed—lives ultimately left to carry the weight of outcomes never chosen.

In full honesty, I didn't know Sergeant Barrett very well. We had only talked a few times, and he seemed like a dedicated, passionate soldier and a stand-up guy. Still, he was a teammate and a brother-in-arms.

This was another event that pulled things back to a grim reality.

That day, a boulder found its way into my rucksack.

It wasn't invited—and damn, I wish it had never shown up.

But I had to carry it in my own way. My reality. My grief. My experience.

> *"It could have been me."*
> *"It could have been any one of us."*
> *"Maybe tomorrow."*

Everyone who carries the weight does so in their own way.

If you've never been deployed, this isn't just another war story—it's the reality of what everyone in high-stress roles faces. Regardless of the color of your uniform, losing someone from your crew hits deep.

We go through the motions physically, but the emotional weight doesn't leave. Unless we acknowledge it, it settles in our rucksack.

Some of it builds up over time—and some arrives in one fell swoop.

CHAPTER 3 ACTION STEP: SHARING THE STORY THAT STICKS

- Recall one incident that still lingers in your mind.
- Write briefly what happened, how you felt then, and how you feel now.
- Share with one trusted peer—weight doesn't lighten by staying in your rucksack.

CHAPTER 3 FIELD NOTES:

Loss in our line of work isn't just personal—it ripples through the entire team. One moment can change everything, and everyone feels it, whether they say it out loud or not. Chapter 3 is about those moments that don't let go. The ones that replay, stick, and follow you long after the mission is over.

Ignoring it doesn't make it easier. It just pushes it deeper, where it starts to show in other ways, like short tempers, distancing yourself from others, poor decisions, or burnout. Acknowledging it doesn't mean you're weak. It means you're dealing with it before it deals with you. Talking about it, even a little, takes some of the weight out of your rucksack and keeps it from breaking you—or the people standing next to you.

CHAPTER 4
MAINTAINING THE RUCK
WHAT KEEPS YOU GOING

"Somewhere inside, we hear a voice.

It leads us in the direction of the person we wish to become.

But it is up to us whether or not to follow."

PAT TILLMAN

In our line of work, it's second nature to make sure everyone else is okay—our coworkers, our families, even strangers—without a second thought. We rearrange schedules, skip meals, and put our own plans on hold to meet other people's needs. Yet when it comes to our own well-being, we often wait weeks, months, or even years before doing anything about it.

However, if we want to perform at our best—whether at home, on a call, in the field, or behind our desks—we must prioritize ourselves first. Just like you wouldn't send a piece of equipment into service without maintenance or put a dirty pistol back in your duty belt and expect it to fire perfectly, you can't expect your mind and body to perform well if you don't take care of them. Yet we walk into high-stress situations running on fumes and call it "part of the job."

There are many things we can do for ourselves, but three stand out as the most important.

EXERCISE – TRAINING FOR THE MISSION, NOT THE SELFIE

Exercise isn't about getting shredded for Instagram. If that's your thing, more power to you. But the real point is keeping the machine running when the job throws hell at you. Regular movement lowers cortisol, the body's primary stress hormone, while boosting serotonin and dopamine—brain chemicals tied to mood, motivation, and focus. Research supports this: exercise regulates these neurotransmitters and stress hormones in ways that directly combat depression, anxiety, and burnout.[1]

An analysis from *Biopsychosocial Science and Medicine* found that exercise can produce effects similar to antidepressant medication.[2] In other words, a powerful, all-natural antidepressant is available to you —but it requires the will and discipline to maintain a regular exercise routine.

You don't need to train like a Navy SEAL. Thirty minutes of walking, lifting, rowing, or cycling four to five days a week is enough to keep you faster, stronger, and sharper than the guy who "doesn't have time," but somehow finds three hours to binge-watch Netflix. Think of exercise as daily armor for your mind and body.

When you skip workouts because you're "too busy," you're just making it easier for stress to kick your ass. You wouldn't run into a fire without your turnout gear—so why run to the next critical call without your body and mind ready? You don't need to be at the gym for three hours every day, but you do need to be consistent.

As author James Clear says, "You do not rise to the level of your goals. You fall to the level of your systems."[3] A consistent thirty-minute workout will beat a heroic three-hour session that leaves you burnt out for a week. Resilience isn't built in one massive effort. It's built rep by rep, shift by shift.

NUTRITION AS AMMUNITION

There are a million books on nutrition, and I won't get into the weeds here, but we need to fuel our bodies like we expect them to perform under pressure—because that's exactly what we expect them to do. Don't get me wrong, I love a good pizza or taking my kids out for ice cream. There's nothing wrong with that in moderation. But living on coffee, energy drinks, and whatever's in the vending machine or on the rollers at the local gas station is like putting cheap fuel in a high-performance engine—your body will sputter, stall, and break down when you need it most.

Our bodies are the only vehicle we have to get through this life. Balanced meals with vegetables, lean protein, and healthy fats stabilize blood sugar, keep your mood steady, and improve your ability to think clearly when things go sideways.[4]

Research from Harvard University suggests that nutrient-rich diets are associated with better emotional control and improved decision-making under stress.[5] No one is saying you can't grab a burger with the crew—just make sure most of the time you're eating in a way that helps you endure in this profession.

You don't need to count every calorie or carry a cooler full of chicken and rice. Focus on consistency and balance over time, not perfection at every meal. If a majority of what you eat is high-quality fuel, the occasional pizza or dessert won't throw you off. Keep healthy snacks in your patrol bag or station fridge, drink more water than anything else, and try to include a fruit or vegetable in most of your meals.

As Dr. Mark Hyman says, "Your fork is the most powerful tool to transform your health and change the world."[6] Small, consistent choices will keep you energized and ready without turning nutrition into a second job.

THE HOME FRONT – GUARDING FAMILY, FREEDOM, AND FINANCES

If your family only sees you exhausted, short-tempered, and staring at your phone, doom-scrolling cat videos, you aren't truly providing. You're just existing in the same house and cashing a paycheck.

Strong relationships and social support are among the most powerful predictors of recovery after trauma. Across 68 different studies, evidence found that post-trauma social support consistently reduces both the likelihood and severity of PTSD.[7]

That means showing up for school concerts, Little League games, family dinners, or relaxing on Sunday afternoons. These moments recharge your body and soul in ways another overtime check never will.

Of course, money matters. Sometimes you need to work hard to pay the bills or reach a goal. But if the grind never stops, you're on a treadmill to burnout. I've seen plenty of guys brag about their massive overtime, and many of them are also divorced, miserable, their kids barely talk to them, and they're counting the days to retirement like it's a prison sentence.

No one will remember how much overtime you worked last summer —except maybe the taxpayers. But your kid will remember you missing their birthday party or dance recital. Your spouse will remember the anniversary you skipped for "just one more shift." Work hard when needed, but don't let the job become your identity.

As Stephen Covey wrote in *The 7 Habits of Highly Effective People,* "The key is not to prioritize what's on your schedule, but to schedule your priorities."[8] Before picking up that extra shift, ask yourself,

> *"Am I adding to my life—or just cashing a bigger check to pay for the damage I'm doing?"*

Maintain a healthy perspective on money. Extra shifts can increase your paycheck, but they won't restore your health, your sanity, or our most precious resource—time.

Your goal should be sustainable performance, not burnout.

ON-THE-SPOT MENTAL SURVIVAL TOOLS

We've hit the key pillars: moving your body, fueling it properly, and protecting the people who matter most. But even if you're doing those things well, life can still catch you off guard. Stress doesn't wait for convenience. It shows up during a call, halfway through a briefing, sitting in traffic after a shift, or lying awake at night replaying what you did or didn't do. That's where these quick tools come in—the ones you can use instantly, anywhere, anytime. They're simple, backed by research, and most importantly, effective.

- **Tactical Breathing (Box Breathing)**

1. Inhale slowly through your nose for four seconds.
2. Hold your breath for four seconds.
3. Exhale through your mouth for four seconds.
4. Hold for four seconds.
5. Repeat for 3-5 cycles.

Why it works: Box breathing activates the parasympathetic nervous system—your body's "calm down" mode. It slows your heart rate, reduces adrenaline, and improves focus. Navy SEALs use box breathing before high-stakes missions to stay composed under pressure.[9]

Evidence: Controlled breathing techniques have been shown to lower cortisol levels and improve cognitive performance under stress.[10]

- **Grounding (5-4-3-2-1 Method)**

  1. Name five things you can see.
  2. Name four things you can touch.
  3. Name three things you can hear.
  4. Name two things you can smell.
  5. Name one thing you can taste.

<u>Why it works</u>: Grounding interrupts racing thoughts by forcing your brain to focus on the present moment. It shifts attention away from the "fight or flight" response and back toward rational thinking.

<u>Evidence</u>: Grounding has been shown to reduce acute anxiety and prevent flashbacks in trauma survivors.[11]

- **Visualization**

  1. Close your eyes and picture a specific scenario—entering a call calmly or delivering a steady, rock-star training brief.
  2. Imagine every sensory detail: sights, sounds, smells, and how your body moves.
  3. Picture yourself succeeding in that moment.

<u>Why it works</u>: Visualization develops muscle memory. Your brain processes vivid mental practice much like real experience, helping you prepare for high-pressure situations.

<u>Evidence</u>: Visualization improves performance in high-pressure situations by 12-20%.[12]

- **Micro-Breaks**

1. Every 60-90 minutes, step away for about one minute.
2. Stretch, walk, or practice box breathing.
3. Avoid your phone—this is mental rest, not distraction.

<u>Why it works</u>: Micro-breaks reduce mental fatigue and boost concentration. They help prevent decision-fatigue, which can degrade judgment during long shifts.

<u>Evidence</u>: Micro-breaks have been shown to maintain "high levels of vigor and alleviate fatigue effectively."[13]

- **Positive Peer Check-Ins**

1. Choose one or two trusted peers you can talk to without fear of judgment.
2. After tough calls or high-stress moments, take a few minutes to decompress together.
3. Keep it mutual—offer support but also accept it.

<u>Why it works</u>: Peer support reduces isolation, normalizes emotional reactions, and strengthens trust within a unit or team.

<u>Evidence</u>: "Formal and informal peer support contribute to post-traumatic growth (PTG) in first responders."[14]

PLAYING THE LONG GAME

Most of us won't be taken out by some freak accident or random catastrophe. Statistically, the real threats are far more predictable. Most people eventually get sick and die from a small group of chronic conditions: cardiovascular disease, neurodegenerative decline, metabolic dysfunction, and cancer.[15]

These enemies don't appear overnight. They're patient. They infiltrate quietly over years—sometimes decades—before anyone notices. The foundation for these diseases is often laid long before we feel sick, when we still believe we're healthy. By the time warning signs show up in our sixties or seventies, the battle has often been underway for a long time.[16]

That means the real battle shouldn't be fought in a hospital room at the end of life, reflecting on what could have been. It should be fought much earlier, in the everyday decisions we make, long before disease shows its face. The focus should shift from reacting to problems once they appear to preventing them in the first place.

For most of us, that means getting serious. The best time to start would have been in your teens or early twenties. If you're reading this book, that ship has probably already sailed. The next best time is *right now*.

Stop thinking about the next thirty days and start thinking about the next thirty years. Do you want to be healthy enough to watch your grandchildren grow up, keep swinging a golf club, keep coaching, or stay mentally sharp enough to enjoy the life you worked your ass off to build?

The formula itself is not complicated, but it does require discipline. Mental health, nutrition, and physical training are the three pillars that support everything else. They reinforce each other, and when one begins to fail, the others aren't far behind.

You get one life. If you want a fighting chance against the enemies that take most of us out, you must start now. Every choice you make today is another item in the rucksack you'll carry for the rest of your life.

Pack wisely.

CHAPTER 4 ACTION STEP: BUILDING DAILY RESILIENCE

- Pick one habit—exercise, nutrition, or family time—to improve this week.
- Pair it with one tool: breathing, grounding, visualization, micro-breaks, or peer check-ins.
- Practice both daily, even during low-stress moments, so they become second nature when pressure hits.

CHAPTER 4 FIELD NOTES:

Self-maintenance matters. You wouldn't send equipment into the field without servicing it—checking it, fueling it, making sure it's ready to do the job. But a lot of people do exactly that to themselves. They run on empty, skip recovery, eat whatever's convenient, and push through without ever stopping to assess the damage. That might work for a little while.

Until it doesn't.

Taking care of your body, what you put into it, and the people closest to you shouldn't be considered extra work. It's part of personal readiness. When you ignore maintenance, the small things don't stay small. Pebbles turn into rocks, and your rucksack gets heavier one day at a time. Staying ready isn't about being perfect. It's about making sure you're not quietly carrying more than you need to.

CHAPTER 5
RECOGNIZING TROUBLE
THE SIGNS YOU SHOULDN'T IGNORE

"When we are no longer able to change a situation,

we are challenged to change ourselves."

VIKTOR E. FRANKL

I f there is one thing we pride ourselves on in this line of work, it's toughness. We *"suck it up and drive on."* We push through exhaustion. We finish the shift no matter how bad we feel. We walk into chaos with steady hands because people depend on us.

The unspoken rule is simple:

Handle your business, and keep moving, soldier.

But toughness has a dark side. It can become a powerful mask. It hides the cracks until they grow so large that the whole foundation begins to fail. By then, fixing the damage is far harder than it would have been if we had stopped early to check.

THE STORY OF FIREFIGHTER "WILL"

We all recognize the type. The Ironman. The guy who never complains, never slows down, never takes a sick day. He seems invincible, no matter what the job throws at him. For the sake of the story, let's call him Will.

Will is a seasoned firefighter-paramedic, built like a linebacker—the kind of guy who can carry a victim down three flights of stairs and still come back for overhaul. He lives for the work. First in, last out. The one everyone depends on.

Will also has a reputation. If you ask him how he was doing, his answer is always the same:

"I'm fine."

And for years, he seemed that way. At least until the cracks began to show.

It wasn't just one call that affected him. It was a series of them—victims he couldn't save, overdoses that blurred together, and dozens of car accidents he can still smell. He brushed them all off. But those incidents stayed with him. The pebbles and rocks were painstakingly accumulating.

At first, the changes were subtle. He stopped going to the gym, even though that had always been his thing. He began skipping meals with the crew, relying on Red Bulls and coffee to get through his shifts. His friends noticed he was quicker to snap, barking at rookies for minor mistakes. At home, he was even shorter with his family. His wife said it was like living with a stranger.

Sleep became an enemy. When he did sleep, nightmares woke him. When he didn't, he lay awake staring at the ceiling or doomscrolling while his mind raced. The man who once joked that stress was for weak people was unraveling—and he was the last to admit it.

It all boiled over one night after a call where a teenager died in a tragic accident. There was nothing Will could do to save her. He returned to the station, slammed his locker so hard it bent, and then disappeared. His Captain found him on the apparatus floor, sitting on the bumper of the engine, his head in his hands, crying uncontrollably. It was the first time he said it out loud:

"I can't do this anymore. I am not fine."

Will wasn't weak. He wasn't broken. He was human. Years of carrying pebble after pebble, a handful of rocks, and maybe a boulder or two had finally pushed him past the point where toughness alone could hold everything together. His rucksack broke.

The same guy who once thought asking for help was a weakness later admitted that the hardest, bravest thing he ever did was walk into his first counseling appointment. Over time, and with support, he found his footing again—not because he was cured, but because he stopped trying to carry his rucksack alone.

Mental strain rarely announces itself with a loud siren. Usually, it gradually creeps in. You skip a meal here, miss a workout there. You stop sleeping through the night. You grow short-tempered with your spouse and kids. Calls that once rolled off your back now linger longer. The fuse shortens, patience thins, and before you know it, you're operating on edge without even realizing it.

The problem is that in our profession, we are trained to ignore these warning signs. That can be admirable when you need to complete an urgent mission or call—but it's a terrible long-term strategy.

If your cruiser's check engine light comes on, you get it looked at.

If your turnout gear is torn, you replace it before the next shift.

If your rifle jams during a firefight, you perform SPORTS and clear it immediately.

But when it's our own head—our own body? Too often, we slap duct tape over the warning lights and "keep on keepin' on."

THE SUBTLE SIGNS

Trouble doesn't always look dramatic. It's not always a textbook case of PTSD or a full-blown panic attack. Sometimes, it's constant fatigue, even on days off. Sometimes, it's a creeping cynicism like, *"Why am I even doing this anymore?"* Or it's the moment you catch yourself staring into space, unable to remember the last few minutes, running on autopilot during the drive home, seemingly detached from reality.

Maybe you've noticed you're quicker to anger. The driver who cuts you off triggers a bigger reaction than they should. The patient complaining about wait times makes you want to snap. The rookie asking dumb questions sends your blood pressure through the roof. That's not really you—it's the weight you're carrying showing up in ways you can't control.

The World Health Organization considers burnout a legitimate occupational issue characterized by three signs: exhaustion, cynicism, and decreased professional effectiveness.[1] If you wake up tired no matter how much sleep you get, catch yourself rolling your eyes during calls, losing motivation, or notice your performance slipping, that's not just a rough patch. Those are your warning lights staring you in the face.

WHEN THE JOB FOLLOWS YOU HOME

One of the most dangerous aspects of all this is that stress doesn't stay at work. It doesn't clock out when you do. If you're carrying too much in your rucksack, it spills over into your personal life.

Think about it. How many marriages in our profession fall apart because work gradually creeps into the home and builds a wall between spouses? How many kids grow up with a parent who is physically present but mentally checked out? How many of us bury ourselves in overtime, claiming we're providing, when really, we're avoiding the hard conversations waiting for us at home?

I've noticed it in myself. After long periods of travel, training, or deployments, I would come home and find my body in the living room, but my mind still at work. My wife and kids would be talking or laughing, and I felt distant, numb, and disconnected. It wasn't that I didn't care. It was that I didn't know how to set the weight down. Often, I couldn't even identify what that weight was.

Studies show that personal trauma often affects people more deeply than occupational trauma. In one study, paramedics were the only group who identified occupational trauma as their worst event, while law enforcement officers, firefighters, and search-and-rescue personnel reported personal trauma as their most distressing experiences. Divorce, the death of someone you love, financial stress—these often become the heaviest burdens we carry. But because they don't happen on duty, we tend to treat them as separate issues.[2]

In reality, they add more pebbles and rocks to the rucksack.

YOUR BODY REMEMBERS EVERYTHING

Even when you refuse to acknowledge it, your body knows what's happening. Trauma doesn't just live in your mind—it lives in your nervous system. It is not something you can simply bury. It embeds itself in you, shaping how you think, feel, and even move.

You might tell yourself you're fine, cover the stress with overtime, or drown it in alcohol, but your body isn't fooled. Eventually, it shows up as insomnia, chronic pain, digestive issues, anxiety, or sudden reactions to minor triggers.

That's why tension builds in your shoulders, or headaches keep coming back. Research shows that unresolved trauma alters the brain's alarm system, rewires stress-hormone pathways, and keeps the body stuck in a state of hypervigilance.[3]

Put simply, you can ignore your mental health for years—but eventually your body will cash the check your mind has been writing.

RISKY COPING MECHANISMS

When the weight in your rucksack becomes too much, we all reach for coping strategies. Some are healthy—exercise, hobbies, time with family. But others only make things worse.

Maybe it starts with a nightly drink to take the edge off that slowly becomes two, three, or four.

Maybe it's the constant overtime—the "I'll just stay busy, so I don't have to think about it," strategy.

Maybe it's adrenaline-seeking—driving too fast, picking fights, or chasing risk because feeling anything is better than feeling nothing.

Avoidance doesn't heal trauma—it deepens it. The American Psychiatric Association identifies avoidance behaviors as a core symptom of

PTSD. The longer you avoid, the worse the symptoms tend to become.[4] It's like covering a bullet wound with a Band-Aid.

WHEN OTHERS SEE IT FIRST

Sometimes the first warning sign isn't what <u>you</u> notice—it's what someone else points out.

> A spouse who says, *"You've been different lately."*
> A coworker who jokes, *"Man, you're crankier than usual."*
> A friend who notices you have gone radio-silent.

It's tempting to brush these comments off, but the people around you often see the cracks before you do. They live with the version of you that you've convinced is fine. When they finally speak up, it isn't nagging—it's them holding up a mirror.

In counseling, there is a concept called the Johari Window. Imagine a window with four panes. One of these panes represents the *blind spot*—the traits or struggles others see in you that you don't see in yourself. Sometimes the people around us see the rocks in our rucksack long before we realize we're carrying them. The Johari Window is less about labels and more about self-reflection, providing a framework for understanding how we present ourselves in the world, and how others perceive us.[5]

Understandably, ignoring others carries real risks. Research on first responders and PTSD shows that stigma and fear of career consequences are among the biggest barriers to seeking help.[6] Yet, ironically, studies also show that early intervention saves careers.[7] It's not the quiet visit to the counselor's office that ends a career—it's the meltdown on duty that no one saw coming. If someone is brave enough to tell you something that you probably don't want to hear, you should take the time to listen and carefully reflect on reality.

CHECK YOURSELF—BEFORE YOU WRECK YOURSELF

So, how can you tell if you're in trouble?

It's simple, but it is often difficult to do some deep soul-searching.

Ask yourself:

> *"Am I more irritable or withdrawn than I used to be?"*
> *"Have my sleep or appetite changed?"*
> *"Do I use alcohol, food, or distractions more than I used to?"*
> *"Do I feel disconnected from my friends, my family, myself?"*
> *"Do I get headaches, stomachaches, or unexplained pain more
>   often than I used to?"*

If the answer to several of these questions is "yes," it's simply a signal that your check engine light is on—and your rucksack is getting heavier.

WHY ACTING EARLY MATTERS

There's a common mentality that you should wait until things calm down before addressing your mental health. But the reality is that life never calms down. There's always another crisis, another call, another emergency. If you wait until the perfect time, you'll be waiting forever—and get nothing done. The job demands that you keep moving, keep responding, and keep pushing, so it's easy to convince yourself that your own pain can wait.

It can't.

Acting early prevents breakdown and protects your relationships, your health, and your ability to continue doing the job you love—the job many of us dreamed about as kids with joy, wonder, and excitement.

Early intervention also stops the quiet erosion that happens long before things look serious. Tension rarely explodes all at once. It chips away slowly—trouble sleeping, shorter fuse at home, avoiding friends, or losing interest in the things that once grounded you.

If ignored, these small shifts harden into patterns that become far harder to reverse, called a "level of embeddedness". Addressing them early is like putting out a small brush fire before it grows into a multi-acre wildfire. It protects careers, families, and the version of yourself you'll want to be in five, ten, or twenty years from now.

Every one of us carries a rucksack. Some days it's light. Other days, it's filled with pebbles and rocks you didn't ask to carry. The danger isn't only the weight itself—it's pretending it isn't there. The strongest people in our professions aren't the ones who never struggle; they're the ones who recognize when the weight is too much and do something about it before it breaks them. That starts with awareness.

CHAPTER 5 ACTION STEP: SPOTTING THE WARNING SIGNS

- Write down three changes you've noticed in yourself over the past six months.
- Ask someone you trust what changes they've noticed in you.
- Share at least one of those observations with a peer, spouse, mentor, or counselor.

CHAPTER 5 FIELD NOTES:

The goal isn't to solve everything in one conversation. It's to recognize when the rucksack is getting heavy—and to stop pretending it isn't. Chapter 5 is about paying attention to the warning signs before they turn into something you can't ignore. The irritability, the sleep issues, the constant chip on your shoulder, the withdrawal from people who you love—those aren't random. They're signals. And if you're honest, most people see them coming long before anything breaks.

Ignoring it doesn't make it disappear, but the straps on your rucksack don't snap overnight. They fray. They stretch. They give you plenty of warning if you are willing to look. Acting early is a part of maintenance. It's how you stay operational, how you protect the people around you, and how you stay in the fight.

CHAPTER 6
THE ROLE OF PEER SUPPORT
WHO'S GOT YOUR SIX?

"I will never leave a fallen comrade."

U.S. ARMY WARRIOR ETHOS

If you've spent time in the military, police, fire, or medical fields, you know one rule by heart: you don't go it alone. In the military, you don't go anywhere without a battle buddy. A police officer wouldn't clear a building without backup, and a firefighter wouldn't advance a hose line without a partner. A nurse doesn't administer high-risk medication without another set of eyes, and a surgeon doesn't operate without a full team in the room. Survival depends on teamwork and trust.

And yet, when it comes to mental health, we break this rule constantly. We'll risk our lives to cover each other on a call, but when the battle happens inside a brother's or sister's mind, we look away. We tell ourselves it's not our business, it's too personal, or that someone else will take care of it.

We stay silent, <u>and that silence is killing us.</u>

THE BROTHERHOOD AND ITS BLIND SPOT

We all take pride in loyalty. The thin blue line, the thin red line, the patch we wear—it signifies that we are part of something greater than ourselves. We say, *"I've got your back."* But too often, that promise doesn't hold up when the struggle is internal.

The signs are easy to spot if we look: the friend who stops coming around, the spouse who can't relax at a family dinner, or the partner who was always squared away—now late, distracted, and disheveled. Everyone sees it. But no one wants to be the one to say something.

We try to rationalize it to diffuse responsibility:

> *"He probably just has a lot going on."*
> *"She's just going through a tough time."*
> *"That's just Carl."*

Ignoring them doesn't help. It allows the problem to grow and quietly exacerbates the behavior.

Research shows what our gut already knows: first responders are more likely to turn to peers when they are struggling.[1] When you have a buddy who has seen and done the same things as you, they are easier to talk to—if we allow it and foster it within our culture. Peer support programs have been shown to reduce burnout and secondary traumatic stress while boosting resilience. In plain English, when we speak up, we give someone a fighting chance. The proverbial olive branch is extended.

WHY PEER SUPPORT WORKS

Peer support works for one simple reason: credibility. When you've stood next to someone on a hot call, sat in the same patrol car at 3 a.m., or deployed with the same unit, there's no need to explain yourself. You don't have to build rapport—they get it. They know the language, the acronyms, the dark humor, and the weight we carry.

Timing also matters. Trauma won't always wait until you're sitting in a therapist's office weeks or months later. Sometimes it hits right after the call, when the adrenaline fades, and the silence creeps in. That's when a quick peer check-in can interrupt the spiral before it hardens into something heavier.

Early intervention, especially peer-driven support, is one of the most effective ways to reduce the long-term impact of trauma. A small conversation at the right moment can change how a memory gets stored—and whether it becomes a pebble or a boulder in your rucksack.

THE STORY OF OFFICER "VICKY"

If a police department is fortunate, it has someone like Officer Vicky on its force. Fourteen years on the job, sharp instincts, quick wit, and steady hands. She's the kind of cop supervisors trust without hesitation. A Field Training Officer (FTO), she has trained half the department at one point or another. Rookies love riding with her because she makes the job make sense. She remains calm under pressure, stays professional without ego, and can read a room better than most detectives.

If you asked her how she was holding up, she always gave the company line:

"Living the dream!"

But she wasn't.

Her rucksack had pebbles. It had some rocks. It had boulders, too. Sexual assault cases that reminded her of her little sister. Welfare checks that turned into body recoveries. A teenage girl who overdosed while her mother watched, screaming hysterically. A car chase that left a driver dead...

Add in the constant hostility on calls, complaints, and residents recording her every move—her rucksack filled quietly but relentlessly.

Her fellow officers noticed the shift in her energy long before she did. She stopped giving her usual thoughtful feedback during FTO evaluations. She skipped meals, worked double shifts, and brushed off anyone who asked how she was doing. Her sarcasm sharpened like a knife. Her patience wore thin. A woman who once went out of her way to help her community now avoided contact with people whenever possible.

She used to love training days. Coaching younger officers through scenarios and stress responses was where she thrived. But one day, she froze during a routine training exercise, unable to make a simple decision, staring at a prop gun as if she had never seen one before. She laughed it off, but the other instructors exchanged looks that silently asked,

"What is going on with Vicky?"

Things were worse at home. She barely slept and kept her vest on long after her shift, sitting on the couch scrolling through her phone. She snapped at her husband for asking simple questions. She avoided school events for her kids because crowded auditoriums felt like death traps and made her feel out of control. She also stopped going to the gym—the one place where she always went to clear her mind.

Nobody said anything. Not because they didn't care, but because this was Vicky we were talking about—the pillar of professionalism, the fixer, the trainer, the one who didn't need help.

Then the call came that broke her. A multi-car accident involving a drunk driver and a minivan. Inside the minivan were three kids—two injured and one who didn't make it. Vicky rode with one of the surviving children to the hospital, holding her hand as she drifted in and out of consciousness, repeatedly asking if her brother was okay.

Vicky didn't go back to the station after that. She drove to a quiet spot overlooking the ocean and sat there for hours, staring blankly at the water, her weapon still on her hip. She never removed it from the holster, but the thoughts running through her mind scared her to death.

What stopped her spiraling thoughts wasn't a dramatic intervention or a perfectly timed conversation with textbook words. It was a simple message from an officer she rarely spoke with outside of work.

> Hey Vicky - that call was horrible, and I'm really worried about you. I'm not judging, but you've been off lately. I just wanted to check in. I'm around if you want to talk.

At first, Vicky was annoyed. Then it cracked something open—a small window of opportunity she allowed herself to step through. She texted back four words she had never said to anyone.

> I'm not doing well.

That one message turned into a coffee. The coffee turned into a peer-support referral. From there, Vicky met with a Licensed Mental Health Counselor who specializes in first responders—someone who didn't flinch at the gallows humor or blunt honesty.

It wasn't an instant fix. She resisted, canceled sessions, argued with her therapist, and sometimes convinced herself she didn't need it. But eventually, she began unpacking the pebbles, rocks, and boulders that she had been dragging behind her for years.

Today, Vicky still has heavy days, but she's now a newer version of her old self—leading training exercises, coaching rookies, and being present with her family. More importantly, she's honest with herself and with others when someone asks how she's doing.

She knows that silence almost cost her everything, and now she has a new message to share with her people:

You don't have to hit the breaking point before you speak up.

And if you see someone slipping, just say something.

That's the job, too.

HOW TO ACTUALLY CHECK ON YOUR BUDDY

This is where most of us freeze. We're trained to act under fire, but when it comes to asking someone how they're <u>really</u> doing, we lock up. It's hard. We don't want to say the wrong thing. We don't want to be awkward, so we say nothing—and nothing is worse than awkward.

Here's how you can check on your buddy in ways that actually work:

1. **Notice and Name It**

Start by pointing out what you see. Keep it simple and direct. Get to the point and don't sugarcoat it.

> *"You've seemed quiet the last few days—everything ok?"*
> *"You've been drinking a lot more lately. What's up?"*
> *"I noticed you haven't been to the gym in the last week. Are you feeling alright?"*
> *"Hey, man – that's your fourth Monster today, what's going on?"*

Naming the change shows the person you're paying attention. You don't need a diagnosis—just a genuine observation that someone sees them and cares enough to say something.

2. **Make it Casual**

Big sit-downs can feel like interrogations or formal interventions.

Instead, keep it low-key.

- Grab a coffee after shift (or during if you can).
- Offer to do a workout together
- Sit in the cruiser or rig for a few extra minutes after a call.
- Start a conversation during your report-writing

3. **Ask, Don't Assume**

Use open-ended questions, not accusations.

> *"How are you holding up after that last call?"*
> *"What's been on your mind? Seems like there's something
>   going on."*

Avoid labels like *"you're depressed"* or *"You've got PTSD."* Accusations push people away instead of inviting conversation. Stick with curiosity, not bold assumptions.

4. **Shut Up and Listen**

This is the hardest part. We are fixers by nature (especially men), but when someone starts talking, the best thing you can do is stay quiet. Don't rush to fill the awkward silence. Don't jump in with advice or a solution.

> *Just. Listen.*

A helpful trick is to repeat the last thing they said in your own words. It shows you're tracking the conversation and really listening.

> Them: *"Man, I can't sleep anymore."*
> You: *"Sounds like your nights have been brutal. What else is
>   going on?"*

5. **Share, Don't Hijack**

Sharing a piece of your own struggle can help normalize theirs. Saying something like *"yeah, after my deployment, I was a mess for a while,"* shows that they are not alone. But don't turn it into a monologue about your own war stories. This is a conversation about them, not you. Offer a glimpse so they know they are not alone, but don't "one-up" the moment.

6. **Keep Checking In.**

The first time you ask, chances are you'll get the brush-off: *"I'm fine."* Take that at face value, but don't walk away and never return. Circle back. Ask again after the next shift or send a text a few days later. Trust isn't built on one check-in—it's built on consistency. When someone realizes you mean what you say and genuinely care, that's when they might start opening up.

7. **Know When to Escalate**

Sometimes, listening isn't enough. If your buddy hints at suicide, harming themselves, harming someone else, or generally being unsafe, you must act. That doesn't make you a traitor—it makes you a lifeline. True loyalty means stepping in, even if it risks the friendship.

If there is any mention of suicide,
get a professional involved immediately.
Call 911, contact the Crisis Line at 988,
or go to your local emergency room.

PUTTING IT ALL TOGETHER

Picture this: you're sitting in your cruiser after a tough domestic call. Your partner hasn't said a word in twenty minutes. Instead of ignoring the tension, you address it directly.

> *"You've been quiet since that last call. That one was pretty heavy. How are you holding up? What's going through your mind?"*

He shrugs it off. You don't push, but you circle back after the shift.

> *"Hey, do you want to grab a coffee? I'll buy."*

While you're sitting there, he cracks the door open:

> *"I've been having a lot of nightmares lately, and it's starting to bother me."*

You don't lecture him or tell him about the latest bio-hack to improve sleep. You don't brush it off with a joke. You listen. Nod your head and say,

> *"Yeah, dude, I've been there. It sucks, but you're not alone in this."*

That's peer support. Not complicated. Not perfect. Just present.

THE MISTAKES WE MAKE

Peer support can save lives, but it can also backfire if handled poorly. Too often, well-meaning conversations shut someone down instead of allowing them to open up. Here are some of the most common mistakes born out of good intentions:

1. **Making a Joke at the Wrong Time**

Humor is part of our culture. It can lighten even the heaviest scenes. But when someone is genuinely trusting you with something personal, a joke sends the message, *"This isn't safe to talk about."* They may never tell you anything again.

2. **Minimizing or Comparing Pain**

Comments like *"Others have it worse than you,"* or *"You think that's bad? Let me tell you about..."* turn support into a competition. Trauma isn't a scoreboard. What weighs on them is real, whether it matches your worst call or not.

3. **Giving Advice Instead of Listening**

Our instinct is to fix problems, but advice can overwhelm or even frustrate someone—especially if they've already tried what you're suggesting. What most people need at that moment isn't solutions. They need to be heard.

4. **Talking About Yourself Too Much**

Sharing your personal struggles can be powerful—it reminds them they're not alone. But if the conversation becomes mostly about your trauma, they'll leave feeling invalidated.

5. **Keeping Dangerous Secrets**

This is a big one. If a buddy talks about suicide or harming others, keeping quiet isn't loyalty—it's dangerous. It could be a death sentence. The right move is to stay with them, show you care, and bring in the appropriate resources. Do not keep this quiet. This needs to go up the chain and to a professional—immediately.

6. **Backing Off After the First Try**

Many people brush you off the first time you reach out. *"I'm fine. Don't worry about me."* If you take that at face value and never circle back, they may see it as proof that you didn't really care. Consistency builds trust.

7. **Making it About Performance**

Some peers try to motivate with statements like, *"If you don't get your shit together, you're going to get someone killed or get fired!"* Framing it as a performance issue adds shame instead of support. What they need is connection, not condemnation. Not from their buddy.

WHY OWNING THESE MISTAKES MATTERS

Think of it this way: when you're clearing a building, one wrong move can put your partner at risk. The same principle applies here. A careless moment can shut the door permanently. A thoughtful, patient approach can open it wide enough to save a life.

Being present doesn't mean you have to be perfect. It means showing up, keeping your mouth in check, and remembering that loyalty isn't silence—it's standing there when it counts.

CHAPTER 6 ACTION STEP: BUILDING A "WATCH-YOUR-SIX" NETWORK

- Notice one peer who seems off this week.
- Ask directly, casually, and without judgment.
- Follow up at least once—don't stop at the brush-off.
- **Escalate immediately** if suicide or safety is involved. Stay with them, remove deadly means if possible, and contact emergency services, **988,** or your chain of command.

CHAPTER 6 FIELD NOTES:

Peer support isn't about perfect words or flawless actions. It's about being there for each other. Watching each other's six doesn't end when the call does, and it includes the unseen battles.

We don't get to choose the calls we face, but we do get to choose how we face them. The job already demands sacrifices that most people will never understand. Don't add silence to that list. Keeping an eye on each other's rucksack means noticing, listening, and standing guard—not just with your body, but with your presence. In the end, it's not programs or policies that save us.

It's people.

CHAPTER 7
PROFESSIONAL HELP
WHEN TO CALL IN BACKUP

"Get humble, or get humbled."

JOCKO WILLINK

O ur professions are stubborn.

Our culture tells us things like:

"Suck it up and drive on..."
"Handle it yourself..."
"Don't bring outsiders in..."
"Don't show weakness..."

In uniform, that mindset works on a call. You rely on training, partners, and muscle memory. But when the enemy is inside your head or your own body, going it alone doesn't work.

It's incremental burnout—or worse.

Most cops, firefighters, medics, soldiers, and nurses know these myths by heart. The stigma still runs deep in our profession.

"I don't want to go talk to a stranger about my feelings."
"Only weak people go to counseling."
"If my department finds out, I'll lose my job."
"Everyone else will think I'm soft."
"No one who hasn't done this job could ever understand."

These myths are powerful. They keep tough men and women trapped in silent suffering, convinced that grit alone will carry them through. But trauma does not fade with time. As psychiatrist Judith Herman puts it, "The ordinary response to atrocities is to banish them from consciousness. But trauma will not be ignored. It will return later as a symptom." Left unaddressed, these issues grow until they begin to dominate your life.[1]

THERAPY ISN'T ONE-SIZE-FITS-ALL

One reason first responders cringe at the idea of counseling is the picture they have in their head—some old stranger in a cardigan asking, *"And how does that make you feel?"* Or a twenty-something with no real-life experience, trying to help process scenes they've never stood in and situations they've never had to live through.

What they don't picture is someone who gets it. Maybe not someone who's done the *exact* same job—but someone who understands the culture, the pace, the expectations, and the dark humor. Or at the very least, someone they trust. Someone they can sit across from without feeling like they have to explain everything from the ground up.

The therapeutic relationship between counselor and client is one of the most important factors for growth and progress.

But that's still only part of it.

You don't just need someone you're comfortable with—you need someone who knows how to help. The tools are just as important. A good therapist brings both. There are hundreds of different approaches to therapy. Some will make sense. Some may not. What matters is finding what actually works for you.

Here are a few worth noting:

- ## Cognitive Behavioral Therapy (CBT)

Think of this as reprogramming your internal fire alarm system. CBT teaches you to identify distorted thoughts like *"I'm worthless,"* or *"It's always my fault,"* and replace them with more accurate ones. It has been proven to be one of the most effective treatments for PTSD, depression, and anxiety.[2]

- ## Eye Movement Desensitization and Reprocessing (EMDR)

Sounds strange, works wonders. By guiding eye movements or other forms of bilateral stimulation, your brain begins to process traumatic memories differently, shifting them from "live ammunition" to "spent rounds." Multiple studies show that EMDR can significantly reduce PTSD symptoms in combat veterans and first responders.[3]

- ## Narrative Therapy

For people who live by story, this method helps you rewrite your own. Instead of being defined by *"the worst call"* or *"that one day in Iraq,"* you learn to place those events within a larger story that still holds hope. Trauma, failure, or painful moments may shape the story, but they don't have to define the ending.[4]

- ## Group Therapy / Peer Groups

Sitting in a room with people who have walked the same ground changes everything. The credibility and rapport are immediate. Groups like Alcoholics Anonymous, Warrior PATHH, or other first responder peer networks prove that healing doesn't have to be a solo act.

Each of these approaches offers different ways to work through what you're carrying—and there are many more. A good therapist will guide you through and adjust along the way.

VICKY'S SECOND CHAPTER

Remember Officer Vicky from earlier? The veteran police officer whose life was gradually unraveling under the weight of the job? The one who sat alone in her car overlooking the ocean after a brutal call, wondering if it was worth continuing? What kept her from slipping deeper into darkness was a simple text from a fellow officer checking in on her. It wasn't dramatic, but it was enough to stop the spiral and give her another day.

What Vicky did next is the part most people don't notice.

The morning after speaking with her fellow officer—still shaken by how close she had come to losing herself—Vicky admitted she couldn't carry her rucksack alone anymore. She reached out to her department's peer-support program and scheduled an appointment with a counselor specializing in first responders. She walked into that session guarded, arms crossed, jaw tight, and ready to hate every minute of it.

But the counselor wasn't some outsider who didn't understand the job. She was a former paramedic who had spent years responding to emergencies before becoming a therapist. She didn't flinch at the dark humor or horrific calls Vicky described. She didn't rush to tell her everything would be okay. Instead, she listened—and gradually began giving Vicky practical tools to regain control of the parts of herself she had lost and lighten the burden she had been carrying for more than a decade.

. . .

Through Cognitive Behavioral Therapy, Vicky learned how she had built a relentless cycle of guilt and self-blame after every call that didn't have a happy ending. With EMDR, they confronted the memory that haunted her most—the crash with the three children. The memory she replayed every night in her head, whether she wanted to or not. These memories still hurt, but they no longer dominated her thoughts. They stopped being the constant soundtrack running in the background of every moment.

Vicky didn't walk out of therapy "fixed", but she did walk out with something she hadn't felt in a long time—hope. Over months of steady sessions, she stopped numbing herself with late-night cocktails. She began showing up for her husband and kids again. She returned to training rookies not because she had to, but because she wanted to help other officers before they reached their own breaking point.

Vicky is still working. She's not perfect, and she doesn't pretend to be. She has heavy days, but she's living proof that these methods can work. She can now carry her rucksack without letting it crush her, and instead of hiding her struggles, she uses them to help others who might need that same lifeline she once received.

HOW TO FIND THE RIGHT THERAPIST

If you're considering professional help, don't walk in blindly. As we've already covered, it's not just about finding someone you connect with—it's about finding someone who can help you carry the weight.

A good clinician knows how to match the right approach to you—your situation, your experiences, and your goals—not just default to whatever they use with everyone else.

Here are some tips on finding someone for you:

1. **Ask peers that you trust.**

Word of mouth is often the best referral. If someone you respect says, *"Yeah, I've been seeing this therapist for months, and they really get it,"* that carries more weight than a hundred Google reviews. Many first responder peer networks maintain informal lists of trusted clinicians. If you're not sure where to start, lean on your brothers and sisters who've already walked down that road.

2. **Check their toolkit.**

Therapists often focus on specific theories or approaches that align with their values, training, and experiences. Some rely heavily on CBT, others on EMDR, and some specialize in trauma-focused group therapy. There are hundreds of techniques and theories in between. Some therapists take a more analytical approach, while others place you in the driver's seat of your own recovery. Ask what methods they use, why they use them, and how those approaches have helped others. If a therapist can explain their approach in a way you understand, that's a good sign. If they dodge the question or dismiss your curiosity, it might be best to look elsewhere.

3. **Look for accessibility.**

Schedules matter. If a therapist can't see you for three months and you're barely holding on, that's a problem. However, many therapists do have full caseloads, which can make it difficult to get an appointment quickly. Fortunately, telehealth has expanded access dramatically since the COVID-19 pandemic. Sometimes the right clinician isn't nearby but can meet with you through a secure video session. Telehealth also eliminates travel and allows you to attend sessions from home. While in-person therapy may still be preferable in some cases, telehealth has proven effective for many people.

4. **Check credentials, but trust results.**

Licenses, degrees, and certifications matter. They show the clinician has training and accountability in the mental health profession. But don't get hypnotized by alphabet soup—clinicians with so many letters after their name, you need a Google search to decode them. There are excellent therapists without fancy titles, and highly credentialed providers or doctors who simply aren't the right fit. The real test is whether you're making progress on your own journey. Are you sleeping better? Drinking less? Snapping at your family less?

If the answer is yes, you're probably in the right place.

5. **Look for cultural competence.**

Can the clinician step into your world without flinching? I've heard stories of highly educated therapists breaking down when a cop shares a call they handled. That's certainly not what you want. A therapist who has worked with first responders understands the difference between bunker gear and body armor. They won't flinch at dark humor or expect you to explain every acronym, jargon, or locker-room talk. When choosing a therapist, ask directly: *"Do you have experience working with first responders or the military?"*

It's not just about the culture of our profession either. Every one of us brings a different background into the therapy room—how we were raised, where we come from, our family dynamics, our values, our race, our experiences with money, authority, and trust. All of that shapes how we view the world and how we carry what we've been through. A therapist should take the time to understand that. They don't assume your experience—they ask, they listen, and they meet you where you are. Because if they don't understand where you're coming from, they're not going to be able to help you get to where you want to go.

6. **Test the fit.**

Think of the first few sessions like a ride-along. You're evaluating whether this person can earn your trust. Do you feel respected—or judged? Are they genuinely trying to understand your world, or just waiting for their turn to talk? You won't know everything after the first meeting, but you'll get a gut feeling. Trust that instinct.

7. **Don't be afraid to fire your therapist.**

If the fit isn't right, move on. Too many first responders stick with a therapist they don't connect with or who doesn't understand the culture. The whole process can start to feel pointless.

Firing a therapist isn't failure—it's ownership.

THE MISTAKES WE MAKE WITH THERAPY

Walking into a therapist's office is no small feat. For many of us, it takes years of carrying the weight, encouragement from a trusted peer, or a moment when the rucksack finally becomes too heavy to ignore. But even after we decide to seek help, we often sabotage the process. The same instincts that keep us alive on the job—control, skepticism, and emotional armor—can follow us into the therapy room. We test the therapist, hold things back, skip appointments, and quit too early. It's rarely intentional, but it happens all the time.

If you know what those traps look like, you can avoid them and give therapy the chance to do its job.

1. **We shop once and quit.**

Many first responders try one therapist, don't connect, and assume, *"Therapy doesn't work."* That's like having one bad field training officer and judging the entire profession based on that experience. Finding the right therapist is like finding the right partner—you need trust, chemistry, and respect. It might take a few tries.

2. **We ghost.**

Skipping sessions, canceling at the last minute, or failing to follow through—it's one of the most common pitfalls. Imagine a rookie firefighter skipping half his training burns and then panicking in a real fire. That's what it looks like when you half-ass therapy. Healing requires repetition and consistency. The steady work, week after week, is what rewires your brain and creates lasting growth.

3. **We expect quick fixes.**

Attending three therapy sessions and expecting a total transformation is like going to the gym for a month and expecting to look like The Rock. Positive changes take conditioning, time, and commitment. Especially with trauma, progress is slow and layered. It doesn't get fixed in one shot.

4. **We wait until crisis mode.**

Think about the person who refuses to see a doctor until they're doubled over in pain. We do the same with mental health, waiting until the night we are in complete crisis mode. Therapy isn't just for the brink of collapse. Like routine maintenance on your gear or regular exercise, the earlier you start, the stronger you'll be when the bad calls come. Often, by the time many first responders ask for help, they're already standing at the edge of the cliff.

5. **We treat therapy like punishment.**

Some departments require counseling after critical incidents. That's a good idea in theory, but it can have unintended consequences. People begin to see therapy as a discipline, like being called to the Captain's office. Therapy is an <u>opportunity</u>, not a punishment. You're learning how to stay in the fight longer and stronger. Changing that mindset matters. You're not in trouble—you're investing in your survival.

6. **We lie and hide things from our therapist.**

This one is brutal but true. Some of us make it all the way to the therapist's office and still hold back details or offer a cleaned-up version of what's really going on. *"Yeah, some of the calls are kind of tough – I'm a little stressed out."* Meanwhile, you're drinking a pint of whiskey and clearing all the rooms in your house before you go to bed. The lie may feel safer in the moment, protecting you from vulnerability or shame, but it robs you of the help you came looking for. A therapist can't treat the ghost of the truth, and they aren't mind-readers. Brutal honesty may feel uncomfortable, but it's the strongest move you can make in that room.

THIS IS WHY IT MATTERS

You can't muscle your way out of PTSD. You can't out-drink depression. And you can't white-knuckle anxiety into peace and silence.

Eventually, the rucksack becomes too heavy. If you ignore it long enough, it will break. With the right professional tools, though, you have hope. Therapy helps you unload some of that weight.

Somewhere right now, a veteran or first responder is sitting alone in a cruiser, a bunkroom, or a quiet corner of their house, wondering if their rucksack will ever get lighter.

It can. But only if we stop pretending that we must carry everything ourselves.

Help exists.

People care.

And the moment you decide to reach for it may be the moment everything begins to change.

CHAPTER 7 ACTION STEP: CHOOSE YOUR WEAPONS

- Think about three things you would want in a therapist: Examples might include someone who understands first responder culture, offers flexible scheduling, provides specific training, or simply makes you feel comfortable enough to talk.
- If inclined, ask a trusted peer whether they have ever worked with a therapist they would recommend.
- Commit to scheduling one appointment. Treat the first session like a recon mission. You are evaluating fit, not signing a lifetime contract.
- If you are having thoughts of suicide or an immediate crisis, escalate immediately. Call or text **988**, contact peer support, or notify emergency services.

CHAPTER 7 FIELD NOTES:

Professional help should not be a last resort.

As we say in the military, it's a **force multiplier**.

Therapy, in its many forms, doesn't erase scars or make the job less brutal. It gives you the weapons and armor to carry the rucksack without the weight of all the pebbles, rocks, and boulders. The myths about weakness are just noise, and they've cost too many brothers and sisters their lives. Therapy turns silent suffering into action and progress.

The first responders who step up to get help are the ones who find a way forward, reconnect with their families, and return to their jobs with clarity, rediscovering the best version of themselves. You can't win these battles alone. Strength means knowing when to call in backup—and then having the courage to do it.

CHAPTER 8
LEADERSHIP'S LOAD
WHAT LEADERSHIP LOOKS LIKE UNDER WEIGHT

"The day your soldiers stop bringing you their problems

is the day you have stopped leading them."

GEN COLIN POWELL, U.S. ARMY

Culture flows downhill. So does bullshit. And if you're the one at the top, you're responsible for both.

The way leaders think, speak, and act sets the tone for an entire unit, team, or department. If the boss says, *"We take care of our people here,"* that order should become law. If a Captain shrugs off stress, the Lieutenants stop checking in. When a Sergeant cracks jokes about weakness, rookies quickly learn to keep their mouths shut. Leadership is never neutral. It either fosters a culture of trust and strength or perpetuates one of silence, struggle, and collapse.

**If you hold rank:
Chief, Colonel, Captain, Lieutenant, Sergeant, or
senior firefighter or officer—
this chapter is for you.**

Many supervisors still believe in dangerous myths:

> *"If they need help, they'll ask."*
> *"My job is tactics and training, not therapy."*
> *"It's just a few weak ones; the strong will carry the rest."*

These beliefs are easy to adopt because they diffuse responsibility away from the leader and onto someone else. But they are false—and they can be deadly. Most first responders will not ask for help until they are already near their breaking point. Their training teaches them to prioritize the team, push through pain, and treat vulnerability as shameful. By the time someone finally knocks on a supervisor's door and says, *"I'm not fine,"* the damage is often already done. That is why effective leadership in this field must be proactive, deliberate, and ongoing. Waiting for a crisis to occur is simply too late.

MODELING STRENGTH AND VULNERABILITY

Departments where leaders openly discuss stress and counseling see higher use of support services and less stigma around mental health. The most influential leaders model openness themselves. When a Chief tells the team, *"I saw a counselor after that call,"* or when a Captain admits that nightmares are part of her reality, it breaks the silence. It shows everyone that seeking support is okay. These leaders do not talk about mental health in abstract terms. They lead by example, setting a standard others feel safe in following.

The same pattern appears in the military. Commanders and senior non-commissioned officers who acknowledge their own struggles report stronger unit cohesion and trust.[1] The message is clear: people follow the example you set, not the slogans hanging on your office wall.

Leaders can't remove every rock from the rucksack—but they can decide whether their people carry it alone.

PROTECTING REST AND RECOVERY

Another key responsibility of leadership is protecting rest and recovery with the same seriousness as readiness. Too many supervisors reward the eighty-hour hero—the one who never takes leave and always volunteers for extra shifts. That culture of constant grind slows performance and accelerates burnout. Exhaustion does not build resilience. It destroys clarity, patience, and sound decision-making.

Sleep-deprived first responders can show impaired judgment, slowed reaction times, and reduced situational awareness—effects similar to being legally intoxicated.[2] In a profession where lives depend on clear thinking and quick decisions, fatigue is not just a personal issue.

It's a safety issue.

Some departments have begun to change this culture. In certain firehouses, mandatory downtime is enforced after pediatric fatalities or other traumatic calls. These policies are not luxuries—they are lifelines. Leaders who recognize that rest is part of readiness send a powerful message: health and safety matter. Leaders who ignore this reality eventually watch careers, and sometimes lives, fall apart.

BUILDING SAFE CHANNELS FOR SUPPORT

Even when rest is protected and leaders model vulnerability, many first responders will still hesitate to come forward. Fear of career consequences is real, and the stigma surrounding mental health remains strong in our profession. That is why leaders must build multiple trusted channels for support. Peer support teams need proper training and active participation. Department chaplains should be visible and engaged. Embedded clinicians must understand the first responder culture to build credibility and trust.

It is not enough to hand out a pamphlet for the Employee Assistance Program and call it a day. In many agencies, EAPs and other similar support systems can still be viewed as a career-killer—something you only use when the rucksack is already broken.

I know, because I've waited too long myself.

In 2003, I was hired as a corrections officer. It was my first step into the law enforcement journey I had dreamed about as a kid. I went through the academy early in 2004, but then received orders to deploy to Iraq with the Army in June. When I returned to work almost two years later, nothing was the same. The department had moved to an entirely new facility, and I already felt like a complete outsider.

But the bigger change was within me.

I did not have the insight or language for it at twenty-three years old, but I was carrying significant trauma—PTSD from Iraq that I believed I could bury and push through.

I walked back into that jail, determined to prove I was fine, even though my body felt like it was on fire every time I pulled into the parking lot. One day, not long after my return, the prison doors locked behind me as I stepped into a pod with seventy-two inmates.

My chest sank.

That familiar, suffocating feeling took over my body—the same sense of being trapped I'd felt overseas. Only now, there was no mission. No war. No rockets, mortars, or IEDs. Just the weight.

I panicked—
Chest pounding. Short of breath. Sweating.
I felt like I was going to die.
My rucksack snapped.

I called my leadership, broke down, and finally said the words I had been avoiding:

"I'm not okay."

That was the last time I ever set foot in that jail.

And it took me another five years to fully understand what that moment meant...

Strength is not pretending you're okay when you are falling apart.

Leaders need to understand how often this moment happens—and how preventable it can be. I don't carry any resentment toward the people there. That was my fight, and they did the best they could with the tools they had and someone they barely even knew. There was one lieutenant there that day who got it. I don't even remember her name, but I've never forgotten how she handled that situation.

Over time, that experience shaped how I look at leadership. It's not enough to have programs on paper or to simply say support is available. It has to be real. It has to meet people where they are—before things get to the breaking point.

Collectively, we need to reduce stigma. Peer-support teams need proper training. Chaplains and supervisors should walk the halls and ride along with crews. Clinicians need to be involved and understand our language and culture. Leaders need to model vulnerability. When support is woven into the fabric of a unit or department rather than added as an afterthought, people do not have to wait until they are broken before asking for help.

Leaders who invest in these lifelines are not just protecting careers...

They are saving lives.

TRAINING BEYOND GUNS AND GEAR

Leadership should also require training that goes beyond the job's technical skills. First responders spend countless hours drilling weapons, tactics, and procedures, yet regular training on stress management, burnout, and trauma resilience still receives far less attention. That imbalance is a mistake.

Mental readiness should be trained with the same seriousness as physical readiness. The mind is the piece of equipment that must function under the most extreme pressure, yet it is often the least maintained.

Fortunately, progress is being made. Some academies now teach recruits tactical breathing after live-fire exercises and integrate stress regulation into marksmanship training. Others have added mandatory mental health first aid and suicide prevention training to annual recertifications.

These practices do more than teach skills—they can change culture. But they also need to be done right. When stress control and mental readiness are treated as core competencies, the stigma begins to weaken.[3]

RESPONDING AFTER CRITICAL INCIDENTS

When tragedy strikes, the eyes of every soldier or first responder turn to their leadership. What leaders do in those critical moments will resonate for years and shape how they are viewed by their people.

· · ·

A memo or a half-hearted speech at roll call is not leadership. Real leadership means showing up, acknowledging the pain, and standing beside your people long after the initial shock fades.

The best agencies build structured follow-up after critical incidents: a debrief within twenty-four hours, another at one week, and another at one month. Counselors remain available on-site as long as needed, understanding that trauma develops in waves, different for each person.

These departments also support families by helping arrange childcare and managing the practical logistics that can become overwhelming after a tragedy. When leaders step up in these moments, they prove that *"we take care of our own"* is not a slogan—it is a commitment.

THE POWER OF LANGUAGE

Words shape culture. Casual comments like *"suck it up"* may seem harmless, but they can close doors permanently. First responders hear those words and think,

> *"If I admit how I feel, I'll be judged."*

The opposite is also true. Simple phrases like *"we've got your back"* create space for honesty. Leaders must recognize that every word they use either lightens the rucksack or adds another pebble.

MEASURING WHAT MATTERS

Finally, leadership must also focus on the right metrics. Too often, success is measured by overtime hours, arrests, tickets, budget wins, or calls handled. Those numbers matter—but they are not the whole picture.

The real health of an organization is reflected in other indicators:

- **Retention:** Are people staying, or are they burning out and leaving?
- **Sick leave:** Are absences rising in ways that suggest stress & fatigue?
- **Peer support usage:** Are your people utilizing available resources?
- **Counseling engagement:** Are these services being used—or avoided because of stigma?

These indicators reveal the true state of an organization's health. Leaders who ignore them miss warning signs and invite crisis.

THE COST OF SILENCE

The silence of leadership has a cost. Every time a Chief dismisses stress, every time a Captain ignores a broken marriage, every time a Sergeant jokes about someone's drinking problem, the damage grows.

Leadership is tested long before a crisis hits. It is tested in the culture you build every day—in the words you choose, the rest you protect, the support systems you create, and the example you set. Your people are always watching. They learn what matters by what you tolerate, what you reward, and what you ignore.

**Leadership is not about
carrying the rucksack for your people.
It's about making sure they don't
have to carry it alone.**

CHAPTER 8 ACTION STEP: LEADING WITHOUT ADDING WEIGHT

- **Protect time off:** Enforce rest after major incidents and stop rewarding those who burn themselves out trying to prove loyalty.
- **Create safe channels for support:** Ensure responders have multiple, trusted ways to seek help without fear of career consequences.
- **Train the mind like you train the body:** Integrate resilience, stress regulation, and trauma awareness into academies and annual training the same way you train tactics and firearms.
- **Show up when it matters:** After critical incidents, be physically present. Support your crew, support their families, and remain engaged long after the first shock fades.
- **Track the right indicators:** Monitor retention, sick leave, and support-service usage with the same seriousness you track arrests, calls, and tactical performance.

CHAPTER 8 FIELD NOTES:

Leadership either adds or removes weight from the rucksack. Every word you speak, every policy you enforce, and every example you set either strengthens your people or quietly pushes them closer to the breaking point.

The question is simple:

Will your leadership make the rucksack heavier—or lighter?

Choose carefully. Lives depend on it.

PUTTING IT ALL TOGETHER

WHEN IT MATTERS MOST

"Each person's grief is as unique as their fingerprint.

But what everyone has in common is that no matter how they grieve, they share a need for their grief to be witnessed."

DAVID KESSLER

There are moments in this line of work that no amount of training or experience can fully prepare us for.

A line-of-duty death
A soldier killed in action.
A suicide within the ranks.
A tragic call that claims the life of a child.
A school shooting.
A fatal fire.

These are not just "bad days." These are seismic events that ripple through entire units, departments, and communities. They can shake identities, fracture trust, and make even the most seasoned responders question whether they can keep going. These stay with you long after the incident is over.

These are the boulders.

INDIVIDUAL TACTICS: STABILIZE THE GROUND BENEATH YOU

In the immediate aftermath of a tragedy, the body floods with adrenaline, grief, and often disbelief.[1] Clear thinking becomes difficult when your nervous system is locked in overdrive. This is where the tools we discussed earlier become essential.

- **Breathe before you move.**

In the fog of shock, the body wants to panic or shut down. Tactical breathing helps regain control. It will not erase the pain, but it can slow the body down enough for you to deliberately make the next, right move.

- **Stick to routines.**

Sleep may be difficult, and appetite may change, but maintaining basic routines is crucial. Eat at consistent times. Walk the dog. Go to the gym. These basic activities remind you that your body is still functioning even when your heart and mind are shattered.

- **Write it down.**

Trauma tends to replay in the brain, looping thoughts repeatedly. Writing those thoughts down—even in blunt, simple sentences—can help unload the mind. It creates distance from the event and allows you to revisit it on your terms instead of the brain's endless replay.

Individually, these tools may feel small. But in the first days after a disaster, they can be the difference between collapse and survival. Think of them as a tourniquet applied in the field—temporary stabilization until more help arrives.

PEER SUPPORT: NOBODY SHOULD CARRY THE WEIGHT ALONE

Service in uniform is never an individual effort. When tragedy strikes, the burden spreads across the entire team. Think back to my story about Sergeant Barrett being killed in action and the heaviness that settled over Camp Phoenix. One person's loss affects everyone who wears the patch or badge, carries a radio, or shares the shift.

In these moments, peer support is not optional. It is vital.

- **Show up.**

After a critical incident, people often instinctively give others their "space." But what most need during those moments is presence. Sitting beside someone in silence, bringing coffee to the station, or simply standing nearby ready to talk sends a clear message: *"You are not alone."*

- **Watch for signs.**

Survivor's guilt, irritability, increased drinking, and withdrawing from friends are not good coping mechanisms. These may be signals that someone is severely struggling. Peers are uniquely positioned to notice these changes. Saying something—even if it feels awkward—may be the moment that helps save a life.

- **Check back later.**

The first week after a tragedy, everyone is present—family, media, colleagues, chaplains. But grief does not follow a calendar. Weeks and months later, the silence can still be deafening. Peer support means reaching out again when everyone else seems to have moved on. A simple text, knock on the door, or a *"Hey, how are you really doing?"* can help prevent someone from sinking deeper into isolation.

**When a flag-draped casket is carried,
it takes many shoulders.
Surviving tragedy is no different.
No one should bear that weight alone.**

PROFESSIONAL HELP: BRINGING IN REINFORCEMENTS

There comes a point when individual tools and peer support are no longer sufficient. The severity of trauma resulting from critical incidents such as fatal fires, school shootings, mass casualties, catastrophic natural disasters, and others often necessitates the involvement of trained professionals—people who can guide recovery, normalize reactions, and offer strategies that peers cannot.

When that level of support is needed, these are good places to start:

- **Critical Incident Stress Management (CISM) Teams**

Properly trained CISM teams conduct structured defusings—short conversations within hours of the incident—and formal debriefings within the following days. These sessions reduce isolation, validate reactions, and create space for responders to process what happened. When done correctly, they help reduce long-term burnout and trauma.

- **Chaplains and clergy.**

For some responders, faith provides the only framework that makes sense of tragedy. Chaplains often serve as cultural translators—people who understand life in uniform while offering spiritual guidance. They are especially important when families are involved, helping bridge the gap between the department and those grieving.

- **Therapists and clinicians.**

Trauma-trained clinicians—particularly those experienced with first responders—can provide a broad range of evidence-based treatments that work. These approaches help responders process traumatic events rather than carry them indefinitely.

Having these resources identified before a crisis occurs is essential.

**Professional help does not mean weakness.
It means reinforcements have arrived.**

LEADERSHIP: SETTING THE TONE IN THE STORM

When tragedy strikes, all eyes turn to leadership. Chiefs, Captains, Commanders, shift supervisors—your presence or absence defines the department's response. Culture is never more visible than in these moments.

- **Be present.**

Leaders must show up—at the station, at the hospital, or at the funeral home. Presence matters far more than having perfect words. Your people will remember whether you stood by them or disappeared when it mattered most.

- **Communicate early.**

Rumors grow in silence. Honest updates—even incomplete ones—are better than hallways filled with quiet speculation. Leaders who speak truthfully while acknowledging the pain build trust at the very moment when trust is most fragile.

- **Give permission to grieve.**

Uniform culture often sends the message: *"move on, tough it out, get back to work."* After a tragedy, leaders must deliberately push against this instinct. Saying *"It's okay to hurt, and it's okay to get help,"* normalizes a human response to loss.

- **Prioritize rest.**

The instinct to jump right back into the job can be dangerous. Leaders should allow recovery time, adjust schedules, and resist the pressure to pretend everything is normal. Exhausted, grieving responders are more likely to make mistakes.

**Leadership cannot erase loss.
But it can determine whether a department fractures
or binds tighter together in its wake.**

THE SHARED RUCKSACK

When tragedy strikes, the weight can be unbearable for any one person. But when everyone lifts—individuals using their tools, peers standing side by side, professionals guiding recovery, and leaders anchoring the culture—the rucksack becomes survivable.

The road forward is never easy or quick. But departments can emerge from these moments with deeper trust, stronger cohesion, and a renewed understanding of why the mission matters.

CHAPTER 9 ACTION STEP: CREATING A CRISIS CARD

Every department should have a simple plan for responding when tragedy strikes. In the chaos of the unexpected, people cannot rely on memory alone. A **Crisis Card** is a short reference guide that outlines the immediate steps for stabilizing individuals, activating peer support, bringing in professional resources, and guiding leadership response.

Step 1: Stabilize the Individual

In the first hours after a traumatic event, the goal is to help responders regain enough stability to function.

- Encourage tactical breathing and grounding techniques to slow panic and regulate the nervous system.
- Reinforce basic routines such as hydration, eating, and rest to maintain physical stability.
- Support healthy processing practices such as journaling, prayer, or quiet reflection.

These steps are the emotional equivalent of applying a tourniquet—they stabilize the situation until more help arrives.

Step 2: Activate Peer Support

Peers are often the first and most trusted line of support.

- Peers should reach out immediately. Presence in the first 24-72 hours matters more than having the perfect words to say.
- Follow-up must continue long after the funeral or incident, when isolation often settles in.
- Peers should watch for warning signs and encourage professional help when needed.

Peer support ensures no one is left to navigate tragedy alone.

Step 3: Call in Professional Reinforcements

Some burdens require specialized support.

- Engage Critical Incident Stress Management (CISM) teams quickly to facilitate structured defusings and debriefings.
- Provide access to chaplains or clergy, especially when families are involved.
- Ensure the availability of trauma-trained clinicians who understand first responder culture.

Departments should identify these resources before a crisis occurs, not after.

<u>Step 4: Leadership Sets the Tone</u>

Leadership response shapes how the entire department processes tragedy.

- Leaders show up physically and visibly during the crisis.
- Leaders communicate openly and honestly to prevent rumors and confusion.
- Leaders give explicit permission to grieve and seek help.
- Leaders adjust schedules and workloads to allow time for recovery.

Leadership presence signals that the department stands together.

<u>Step 5: Keeping the Long Game in View</u>

Healing from tragedy takes time.

- Recovery may take months or years, not days.
- Departments should continue offering counseling, peer check-ins, and remembrance events.
- Anniversaries and reminders can reopen wounds; planning ahead prevents responders from facing them alone.

Supporting responders through the long recovery honors both the living and the fallen.

CHAPTER 9 FIELD NOTES:

When the worst happens, survival isn't about toughness or stoicism. It's about recognizing that the weight is sometimes more than you can carry on your own. These incidents hit harder than anything before, and the people who get through are the ones who call in reinforcements—leaning on their team, their families, their support systems, and every tool they've learned along the way.

No one is built to carry this kind of weight alone. Trying to do it by yourself can break you. Know when to reach out, when to speak up, and when to let someone else help shoulder the load.

When it matters most, pain and grief need to be seen and acknowledged by others—not "fixed." Presence, compassion, and giving space to tell their story are essential. This type of grief isn't a problem to be solved. It's a season to be lived.[2]

CHAPTER 10
CARRYING THE RUCK TOGETHER
DON'T CARRY IT ALONE

"The strength of the team is each individual member.

The strength of each member is the team."

PHIL JACKSON

 fter Iraq, I was a mess.

I came home with a body that looked intact—all my fingers and toes accounted for—but my mind was anything but. I didn't want to leave the house. I jumped at shadows. I lived in a constant state of tension —always on edge, always scanning, always waiting for the hammer to drop and something to go terribly wrong. My brain was stuck in a cycle of rumination and hypervigilance. Nightmares pulled me back to the desert. My mind was never at rest.

. . .

I handled it the way I thought a strong man was supposed to handle hard things.

> *I shoved it down.*
> *I tightened up.*
> *I kept moving.*

I told myself that if I could just push through long enough, it would fade.

It didn't.

I thought toughness meant staying quiet. I thought strength meant never letting anyone see the cracks. I convinced myself nothing was wrong while my world slowly got smaller—fewer places I felt safe, fewer people I wanted to be around, and fewer moments I actually felt like myself.

> *I avoided crowds.*
> *I startled easily.*
> *I pulled away from the people who loved me the most.*

I was drowning, and only one person knew.

Fortunately, she married me.

My first step toward healing was not something I chose on my own. My wife saw what I could not—or would not—admit. She watched me struggle under the weight of my rucksack and cared enough to speak up. When I was ready to give up, she pushed me forward.

· · ·

Her belief in me was stronger than my own at that time. Looking back, it's no surprise she eventually chose mental health as her career. Maybe my experience played a small part in that path—but the truth is she was built for this work long before I understood how badly I needed it.

Eventually, I walked into a local Vet Center and met my first counselor. He was a decent guy, but the connection wasn't there. We didn't share common ground, and the sessions felt hollow. I walked out thinking maybe counseling simply wasn't going to work for me. I felt that I had finally built up the courage to try something, only to discover it might be for nothing.

What I didn't understand then is that connection matters. Fit matters. Timing matters. One dead end does not mean help isn't real. It simply means that wasn't the right place to find it.

Over the years, I have worked with a few different therapists. Each one helped in different ways during different seasons of my life.

I have humbly sat across from psychiatrists and taken medication that helped quiet the noise long enough for me to catch my breath and do the work.

Slowly, sometimes painfully, I learned what I had resisted for years.

This wasn't weakness.
This was strength.

That's the story I want to leave you with.

If you take anything from this book, let it be this:

Strength is not found in silence.
It's found in honesty.
It's found in connection.
It's found in the courage to admit that the rucksack
is sometimes too heavy to carry alone.

We openly discuss every other part of our health. A bad knee. A back surgery. High blood pressure. Cholesterol. We swap scars like war stories. But when it comes to nightmares, panic attacks, depression, grief, or the slow erosion that comes from repeated exposure to trauma—we go silent.

The silence does not protect us. It buries us.
Silence is the heaviest thing we carry in the rucksack.

Our line of work puts us face-to-face with human suffering. The world is not suddenly going to become easier. You will continue to see people on their worst days—every day. You will run toward the places everyone else is running from. You will absorb fear, loss, anger, grief, and despair again and again.

That kind of exposure leaves marks. It digs the straps of that rucksack deeper into your shoulders. Anyone who says otherwise is either lying or ignorant.

Carrying around all that weight, over all that time—leads to one final question:

What meaning and purpose will you make from all of it?

I've had nights when I didn't understand what my body was trying to tell me. I've sat through counseling sessions that felt like dead ends. I've swallowed my pride and taken medications I swore I would never need.

But I kept showing up.

Not because I had everything figured out—far from it. But because I knew my story wasn't finished.

And neither is yours.

Whatever it is, that weight is real.
But the rucksack doesn't have to break you.

Maybe it was the child you couldn't save. Maybe it was the crash you can still smell. Maybe it's the moment that keeps visiting you uninvited.

Chances are, you already know exactly which moment that is.

Or—maybe it's the pressure of holding everything and everyone together while quietly falling apart yourself.

There's an idea that renowned psychiatrist Viktor Frankl wrote about after surviving three years in Nazi concentration camps—that even when someone feels finished with life, life may not be finished with them. There is still something to be asked of you. Something that only you can carry forward.[1]

In our line of work, it can feel like the weight has taken everything out of you. Like you've given everything you have to give. But if you're still here—there's a reason.

Maybe it's your family, your faith, or the people you serve. Maybe it's the person you're still becoming, or the things you're still meant to do.

The weight you've carried doesn't disqualify you from that—it may be precisely what prepares you for it.

You've carried it this far. The pebbles, rocks, and boulders that have piled up over the years are real. Some were unavoidable. Most were never yours to choose.

By now, I hope you understand that:

> *You cannot outwork trauma.*
> *You cannot grind yourself into exhaustion and call it strength.*
> *You cannot heal in isolation.*
> *You do not have to become a martyr trying to save the world*
>   *while losing yourself in the process.*

I care about this because I've lived it, and I've watched too many good people convince themselves that suffering in silence is the price we must pay for serving our country or community.

Our jobs already ask enough of us. They should not ask for your life as well.

In the Army, the Field Artillery is known as the *King of Battle*—not because it fights the battle for you, but because it brings overwhelming support when the fight becomes too much to handle alone.

> *Your mental health works the same way.*

You don't call in the artillery because you failed. You call it because you intend to succeed.

Because some battles cannot be won by individual effort alone.

Because coordinated support, brought in at the right moment, saves lives.

The call doesn't have to be perfect.
It doesn't require all the right words.
It doesn't require absolute certainty.
It only requires honesty.

I've carried the rucksack long enough to know the weight is real. And I care enough to tell you, as clearly as I can, that it does not have to break you.

You matter.
Your well-being matters.
Your life matters.

When the weight becomes too heavy to carry on your own, do not disappear into silence.

Silence doesn't make you stronger.

It only guarantees you fight alone.

No one was ever meant to
carry the rucksack alone.
Call in the artillery.
Support will come.

ACKNOWLEDGMENTS

This book was intended to be part field manual, part memoir, and part peer-support workbook. Something like this never comes from just one person. It is the culmination of more than a quarter-century of people who have shaped me, loved me, challenged me, and refused to let me carry my rucksack alone.

First, to my wife, Lauren. I've said it a hundred times, but I still don't know where I would be without you. You have seen me at my worst and still believed there was something worth fighting for in me. You carried your own weight while helping me shoulder mine, and you've built a career doing the same for countless others. Your ability to sit with people in their darkest moments and help them find light never ceases to amaze me. This book would not exist without your strength, wisdom, love, and stubborn refusal to let me quit. I love you.

To my children, Evan and Aria—you are the reason I strive to improve every single day. I am by no means perfect, but you inspire me to be better today than I was yesterday. Every karate practice, baseball game, gymnastics meet, music concert, and every silly moment at home or at the campground reminds me of what really matters. You've taught me that true joy and purpose are not found in rank, badges, titles, or awards—they are found in love, family, and togetherness.

To Mom, Darrell, Nana, Heather, Sandy, and Butch—thank you for being there every step of the way. Every birthday, every holiday, every milestone. It wasn't always easy or pretty, but the love and support you gave made me who I am today.

To my mentors—those who modeled honesty, leadership, and integrity, especially in the face of struggle—thank you for showing me what strength really looks like. Each of you entered my life at the right time, shaping me in ways I still carry with me. I won't list names here, but if I have ever called on you for advice, asked you tough questions, leaned on you for support, cried on your shoulder, or genuinely valued your opinion, consider this my salute to you.

To my brothers and sisters in uniform—military, police, fire, EMS, corrections, dispatch, medicine, and beyond—this book is for you. You walked beside me through deserts and mountains, army bases and firehouses, prisons and police stations. You've had my back, made fun of me when I needed it, and carried me through both laughter and grief. You taught me that loyalty is more than words—it's the quiet, everyday choice to keep showing up for each other. Your stories, your scars, and your sacrifices are the heartbeat of these pages.

To the soldiers I served with in Iraq—thank you for the trust, the humor, and the reminders that even in the worst places on earth, laughter is still possible. To the leaders I worked under in Afghanistan, including those who are no longer with us, thank you for showing me what it means to put people first, even in the midst of chaos.

To my brothers in the 101st Field Artillery Regiment—my first NCOs who showed me the way and my breakfast companions— thank you for being there for me and allowing me to be there for you.

To my firefighting brothers in the 179th and 180th—thank you for showing me a different side of the service. One I didn't even know existed, and one I am proud to say I was a part of.

To my Halifax crew—you know who you are. The O.G. friends I have known my entire life, and the newer ones who stepped in without hesitation. Thank you for being there. Knowing I can trust you with my kids or count on you to answer the phone in the middle of the night is a gift I never take for granted.

To Sergeant Michael Kelley and Sergeant Robert Barrett—your names and your sacrifices will never fade. The weight of losing you never leaves my rucksack, but neither does the pride of having served alongside you.

To the family, friends, and brothers-in-arms whom I have lost along the way, and especially to my father—though you are not here to read these words, your influence and presence remain in the life I have lived and the lessons I have tried to pass on in these pages.

To the readers—whether you picked up this book because you're struggling yourself or because someone you love is—thank you for trusting me with a piece of your story. If even one page helps lighten your load, every hour spent writing this was worth it.

Finally, and above all, to God—who has given me the strength to keep showing up when I thought I had nothing left. When the rucksack felt unbearable, I was never carrying it alone. My faith is not perfect, but it has been a steady compass guiding me through life's storms, reminding me that even in darkness, there is always a light.

When life pressed hard, and the road grew steep, I found shelter I can't fully explain—a calm beneath the chaos. A hand that helped lift some of the weight I thought I might have to carry forever. I've learned that protection does not always mean being kept from the fire. Sometimes it means having the courage to stand in it and keep moving straight through, and the ability to create meaning from it all.

Over time, I've come to trust that I was never walking this path or carrying the weight alone.

A FINAL REFLECTION

Imagine the rucksack each of us carries through life. Some days it holds purpose, responsibility, and the tools we need to move forward. Other days, it fills with things we were never meant to carry alone—fear, stress, grief, anxiety, and the scars left by difficult experiences.

For me, meaning comes from faith, family, togetherness, and service—in that order. But my faith is something I've leaned on when things didn't make sense, when the weight felt heavier than I could carry, or when there wasn't a clear path forward. It gave me something steady—something to hold onto when everything else felt out of control.

What matters is that you find your reason—your *"why."* The thing that gives the weight a purpose. It might be faith. It might be your family, the people beside you, the ideas you turn into creations, the responsibilities you carry, or the community you strive to improve.

The "how" will always change. The "why" is what holds. And when you have that, you can carry more than you ever thought possible.

ABOUT THE AUTHOR

Steve Littlefield is a retired Army Sergeant First Class with over 25 years of military experience, including combat deployments to Iraq and Afghanistan. He has also served in law enforcement and fire services, spending much of his career in environments where stress, loss, and responsibility are part of the job.

He currently serves as a Veteran Service Officer, is completing his graduate degree in mental health counseling, and plans to specialize in working with veterans and first responders. He is the founder of The Veterans Next Step Foundation, a nonprofit dedicated to supporting veterans through mental health services and emergency assistance, and serves as the Operations Manager for The Anchor Within Counseling & Wellness Center, a group mental health practice.

Steve's life and work focus on supporting veterans, first responders, and others who carry the cumulative weight of trauma. *The Rucksack We Carry* was written to put words to that experience and offer a practical way to understand and manage the weight we carry.

For more information, please visit www.therucksackwecarry.com

REFERENCES

AUTHOR'S NOTE

1. Alexander, Caroline. 2010. "The Shock of War." Smithsonian. September 2010. https://www.smithsonianmag.com/history/the-shock-of-war-55376701/
2. National Institute of Mental Health, "Post-Traumatic Stress Disorder (PTSD)," last modified September 2023, https://www.nimh.nih.gov/health/topics/post-traumatic-stress-disorder-ptsd

INTRODUCTION

1. Delony, John. 2020. *Redefining Anxiety*. Ramsey Press.
   Delony, John. 2022. *Own Your Past Change Your Future*. Ramsey Press.
   Delony, John. 2023. *Building a Non-Anxious Life*. Ramsey Press.

1. THE RUCKSACK

1. van der Kolk, Bessel. 2015. *The Body Keeps the Score: Brain, Mind, and Body in the Healing of Trauma*. New York: Penguin Books.
2. Pennebaker, James W., and Sandra K. Beall. 1986. "Confronting a Traumatic Event: Toward an Understanding of Inhibition and Disease." *Journal of Abnormal Psychology* 95 (3): 274–81. https://doi.org/10.1037//0021-843x.95.3.274.

2. IRAQ

1. Genova, Cathleen. 2005. "Scituate Soldier Killed in Afghanistan." The Patriot Ledger. June 20, 2005. https://www.patriotledger.com/story/news/2005/06/20/scituate-soldier-killed-in-afghanistan/40155254007/.

3. AFGHANISTAN

1. Papadopoulos, Maria. 2010. "Soldier Killed from Brockton-Based National Guard Unit." Enterprise News. The Enterprise. April 22, 2010. https://www.enterprisenews.com/story/news/state/2010/04/22/soldier-killed-from-brockton-based/40184502007/.

4. MAINTAINING THE RUCK

1. Heijnen, Saskia, Bernhard Hommel, Armin Kibele, and Lorenza S. Colzato. 2016. "Neuromodulation of Aerobic Exercise—a Review." *Frontiers in Psychology* 6 (1890). https://doi.org/10.3389/fpsyg.2015.01890.

2. Hoffman, Benson M., Michael A. Babyak, W. Edward Craighead, Andrew Sherwood, P. Murali Doraiswamy, Michael J. Coons, and James A. Blumenthal. 2011. "Exercise and Pharmacotherapy in Patients with Major Depression: One-Year Follow-up of the SMILE Study." *Psychosomatic Medicine* 73 (2): 127–33. https://doi.org/10.1097/psy.0b013e31820433a5.

3. Clear, James. 2018. *Atomic Habits: An Easy & Proven Way to Build Good Habits & Break Bad Ones*. New York: Penguin Publishing Group.

4. Polizzi, Stephanie. 2024. "Food and Mood: How Diet Is Key to Mental Health." OSU Extension Service. September 9, 2024. https://extension.oregonstate.edu/catalog/em-9444-food-mood-how-diet-key-mental-health

5. Harvard University. 2023. "Healthy Eating Plate." The Nutrition Source. The President and Fellows of Harvard College. January 2023. https://nutritionsource.hsph.harvard.edu/healthy-eating-plate/.

6. Hyman, Mark. 2018. *Food : What the Heck Should I Eat?*. Little Brown & Co.

7. Ozer, Emily J, Suzanne R Best, Tami L Lipsey, and Daniel S Weiss. 2003. "Predictors of Posttraumatic Stress Disorder and Symptoms in Adults: A Meta-Analysis." *Psychological Bulletin* 129 (1): 52–73. https://doi.org/10.1037/0033-2909.129.1.52.

8. Covey, Stephen R. 2016. *7 Habits of Highly Effective People*. New York: Simon & Schuster Ltd.

9. Kumar, Karthik. 2021. "Why Do Navy SEALs Use Box Breathing?" MedicineNet. MedicineNet. November 18, 2021. https://www.medicinenet.com/why_do_navy_seals_use_box_breathing/article.htm.

10. Ma, Xiao, Zi-Qi Yue, Zhu-Qing Gong, Hong Zhang, Nai-Yue Duan, Yu-Tong Shi, Gao-Xia Wei, and You-Fa Li. 2017. "The Effect of Diaphragmatic Breathing on Attention, Negative Affect and Stress in Healthy Adults." *Frontiers in Psychology* 8 (874): 1–12. https://doi.org/10.3389/fpsyg.2017.00874.

11. Najavits, Lisa M. 2021. *Seeking Safety: A Treatment Manual for PTSD and Substance Abuse*. Guilford Publications.

12. Taylor, Jim, and Shel Taylor. 1997. *Psychological Approaches to Sports Injury Rehabilitation*. Gaithersburg, Md.: Aspen Publishers.

13. Albulescu, Patricia, Irina Macsinga, Andrei Rusu, Coralia Sulea, Alexandra Bodnaru, and Bogdan Tudor Tulbure. 2022. "'Give Me a Break!' a Systematic Review and Meta-Analysis on the Efficacy of Micro-Breaks for Increasing Well-Being and Performance." Edited by Michael B. Steinborn. *PLOS ONE* 17 (8). https://doi.org/10.1371/journal.pone.0272460.

14. Donovan, Nicole. 2022. "Peer Support Facilitates Post-Traumatic Growth in First Responders: A Literature Review." *Trauma* 24 (4): 146040862210794. https://doi.org/10.1177/14604086221079441.

15. Centers for Disease Control and Prevention, *About Chronic Diseases*. Atlanta: U.S. Department of Health and Human Services, 2023. https://www.cdc.gov/chronicdisease/about/index/htm

16. Attia, Peter, and Bill Gifford. *Outlive: The Science and Art of Longevity*. New York: Harmony Books, 2023.

5. RECOGNIZING TROUBLE

1. World Health Organization. 2019. "Burn-out an 'Occupational Phenomenon': International Classification of Diseases." World Health Organization. May 28, 2019. https://www.who.int/news/item/28-05-2019-burn-out-an-occupational-phenomenon-international-classification-of-diseases.

2. Wild, Jennifer, and Tingyee E. Chang. 2022. "Is It Personal? The Effect of Personal vs. Occupational Trauma on PTSD Symptom Severity in Emergency Responders." *Frontiers in Psychiatry* 13 (June). https://doi.org/10.3389/fpsyt.2022.856895.

3. van der Kolk, Bessel. 2015. *The Body Keeps the Score: Brain, Mind, and Body in the Healing of Trauma*. New York: Penguin Books.

4. American Psychological Association. 2021. "Post-Traumatic Stress Disorder." *American Psychological Association*, 2021. https://www.apa.org/topics/ptsd.

5. Gardiner, Kirsty . 2023. "How to Use the Johari Window to Improve Leadership." PositivePsychology.com. August 8, 2023. https://positivepsychology.com/johari-window/.

6. Spitzer, Ashley. 2020. "First Responders and PTSD: A Literature Review - JEMS: EMS, Emergency Medical Services - Training, Paramedic, EMT News. July 28, 2020. https://www.jems.com/mental-health-wellness/first-responders-and-ptsd-a-literature-review/.

7. Litz, Brett T. 2008. "Early Intervention for Trauma: Where Are We and Where Do We Need to Go? A Commentary." *Journal of Traumatic Stress* 21 (6): 503–6. https://doi.org/10.1002/jts.20373.

6. THE ROLE OF PEER SUPPORT

1. SAMHSA. 2018. "First Responders: Behavioral Health Concerns, Emergency Response, and Trauma." *SAMHSA*. https://www.samhsa.gov/sites/default/files/dtac/supplementalresearchbulletin-firstresponders-may2018.pdf.

7. PROFESSIONAL HELP

1. Herman, Judith Lewis. 2015. *Trauma and Recovery : The Aftermath of Violence-- from Domestic Abuse to Political Terror*. New York: Basic Books.

2. Beck, Judith S. 2011. *Cognitive Behavior Therapy: Basics and Beyond*. 2nd ed. New York: Guilford Press.

3. Shapiro, Francine. 2017. *Eye Movement Desensitization and Reprocessing (EMDR) Therapy, Third Edition.* Guilford Publications.

4. White, Michael, and David Epston. 1990. *Narrative Means to Therapeutic Ends.* New York ; London: W.W. Norton & Company.

8. LEADERSHIP'S LOAD

1. Hoge, Charles W., Carl A. Castro, Stephen C. Messer, Dennis McGurk, Dave I. Cotting, and Robert L. Koffman. 2004. "Combat Duty in Iraq and Afghanistan, Mental Health Problems, and Barriers to Care." *New England Journal of Medicine* 351 (1): 13–22. https://doi.org/10.1056/nejmoa040603.

2. International Association of Fire Chiefs. 2013. "The Effects of Sleep Deprivation on Fire Fighters and EMS Responders." International Association of Fire Chiefs, Safety, Health and Survival Section. 2013. https://www.iafc.org/docs/default-source/1safehealthshs/progssleep_sleepdeprivationreport.pdf.

3. Anderson, Judith, Konstantinos Papazoglou, Harri Gustafsberg, Peter Collins, and Bengt Arnetz. 2016. "Mental Preparedness Training | FBI: Law Enforcement Bulletin." FBI: Law Enforcement Bulletin. March 9, 2016. https://leb.fbi.gov/articles/featured-articles/mental-preparedness-training.

9. PUTTING IT ALL TOGETHER

1. Arieh Y. Shalev, Israel Liberzon, and Charles Marmar, "Post-Traumatic Stress Disorder," *New England Journal of Medicine* 376, no. 25 (2017): 2459–2469.

2. Kessler, David. 2020. *Finding Meaning: The Sixth Stage of Grief.* Simon and Schuster.

10. CARRYING THE RUCK TOGETHER

1. Frankl, Viktor E. 1946. *Man's Search for Meaning.* Boston: Beacon Press.